IT Solutions Series

IT Security
Advice from Experts

Lawrence M. Oliva

CyberTech Publishing
Hershey • London • Melbourne • Singapore

Senior Managing Editor:	Jan Travers
Managing Editor:	Amanda Appicello
Development Editor:	Michele Rossi
Copy Editor:	Ingrid Widitz
Typesetter:	Jennifer Wetzel
Cover Design:	Lisa Tosheff
Printed at:	Yurchak Printing Inc.

Published in the United States of America by
CyberTech Publishing (an imprint of Idea Group Inc.)
701 E. Chocolate Avenue, Suite 200
Hershey PA 17033 USA
Tel: 717-533-8845
Fax: 717-533-8661
E-mail: cust@idea-group.com
Web site: http://www.idea-group.com

and in the United Kingdom by
CyberTech Publishing (an imprint of Idea Group Inc.)
3 Henrietta Street
Covent Garden
London WC2E 8LU
Tel: 44 20 7240 0856
Fax: 44 20 7379 3313
Web site: http://www.eurospan.co.uk

Copyright © 2004 by Idea Group Inc. All rights reserved. No part of this book may be reproduced in any form or by any means, electronic or mechanical, including photocopying, without written permission from the publisher.

Library of Congress Cataloging-in-Publication Data

Oliva, Lawrence M.
Information technology security : advice from experts / Lawrence Oliva.
p. cm.
Includes bibliographical references and index.
ISBN 1-59140-247-6 (pbk.) -- ISBN 1-59140-248-4 (ebook)
1. Computer security. I. Title.
QA76.9.A25O64 2004
005.8--dc22

2004005871

British Cataloguing in Publication Data
A Cataloguing in Publication record for this book is available from the British Library.

All work contributed to this book is new, previously-unpublished material. The views expressed in this book are those of the authors, but not necessarily of the publisher.

10

IT Solutions Series:

IT Security

Advice from Experts

Preface

Increasing every day in frequency and sophistication, planned cyber attacks are impacting systems, data and user access at virtually every business and government organization. Whether accidentally triggered by users opening their daily e-mail, or planned denial of services attack triggering a thousand zombie systems, IT management and corporate executives must be ready to respond, minimize and defeat threats to revenue generating and citizen facing operations. In many cases, the decision to protect information assets may materially impact agency or corporate budgets, previously planned investment and projected shareholder returns.

Edited by a senior IT executive with contributions from industry and government experts, this book is written for senior managers by senior managers. Avoiding technical jargon except when necessary, the book is organized into three primary sections of governance, architecture and technology. Each section provides extensive insights, including the legal, staffing, financial, communications, risk, management strategies and technical aspects of securing IT computing and communications systems. A decision framework is provided at the end of each chapter to assist in making the management trade-offs between investment, security, access and legal compliance. At the end of the book are reference lists of publicly available security related information sources.

Using the book's decision trade-off frameworks to make better decisions, executives and managers select which short-term and long-term investments and support activities are required to protect their computing infrastructures. Based on best practices from information assurance professionals and security consultants in government and industry, the unique decision trade-off frameworks describe processes, actions and budgets that effectively protect information and system access in a quickly changing and challenging world.

The **Executive Overview** discusses the *security as a process* concept that has gained recognition within the IT and security communities. Several topics reviewed include the new world of IT security, the continuously increasing value of information assets, and the security challenges and responsibilities facing executives and senior managers today.

Section I reviews the governance issues of IT security, including balancing employee privacy with information access, administrative security policies, legal exposures, risk management strategies and trusting trusted systems.

Section II introduces the architecture issues of IT security, starting with building a threat matrix. It then provides details on architecture alignment with service level agreements, constructing multilevel protection barriers, and revealing internal threats to IT security processes. The section also discusses disaster planning approaches.

Section III focuses on technology issues that intersect and support the issues of governance and architecture. Technology components comprise a large percentage of IT security investments, and executives need some understanding of how the technology is applied, how it functions and why it is so expensive to operate and maintain. This section reviews COTS software protections, data backup and restore, continuity planning, data obsolescence, biometrics, smartcards, and security penetration testing.

Reference Materials are provided as pointers to publicly available information security sources. As major legislative and technical standards are expected in the coming years, checking these sources for updates on a quarterly basis is prudent and beneficial.

Acknowledgments

Books on technology and security are team contributions from both the technical and managerial perspectives. *Information Technology Security: Advice from the Experts* has benefited from editorial review and contributions from numerous experts in the field, who gave generously of their time and knowledge. The following people have provided contributions to, or reviewed all or part of the manuscript: Robert L. Lowry, former Director of Computer Aided Design Services, TRW Inc.; Norman J. Schweitzer, Senior Manager, CATIA Inc.; Douglas Purvance, President & CEO, e-Global Trading Partners; John Whipple, Senior Project Manager, Dell Computer Inc.; Dorothy Nolan, President & CEO of Offix Inc.; Gordon Chastain, President & CEO, SPIN International; Timothy Slusser, CIO & Vice President, CSC Federal Sector; Kevin Kelley, Program Executive, PRIME Alliance; Aaron Phelps, Director of System Test & Operations; Ted Bream, Director for the MeF Project; John McKenna, Director of Systems Engineering Operations, PRIME Alliance Program; Stephen Proctor, Deputy Director, Infrastructure Engineering PRIME Alliance Program; Richard Feucht, Director of Security and Privacy Office, PRIME Alliance Program; and John Boelens, Director of Infrastructure Engineering, PRIME Alliance Program.

To these people and many others I may have failed to give credit to, your ideas, suggestions and guidance over the years have been of the highest value possible and are much appreciated. Any errors or omissions are of course my own. Please advise the author of errors via e-mail at IITSbook@aol.com and I will do my best to correct errata in subsequent versions of the book.

I must also express thanks to the four primary contributors to this book: Chrisan Herrod, Charles Rex IV, Clifton Poole, and Craig E. Kaucher. The quality of their content and responsiveness to deadlines were incredible, given the significant responsibilities they have in their normal duties at the National Defense University in the Washington DC area.

From a senior management perspective, the future of information technology security is equally frustrating and satisfying. Almost every day brings yet another series of reports and requirements detailing security breeches, software patches and system vulnerabilities. It is somewhat frustrating to both executive management and security professionals that whatever defenses are developed, purchased, installed or operated, over time they will be defeated by clever people and misapplied technology components.

However, every day that unauthorized people and intrusive attacks are kept out of information, systems, networks and buildings, and business operations continue without interruption, is professionally satisfying. The objective, of course, is to achieve 100% sustained success in protecting information, systems and networks—a difficult and challenging feat.

Wishing you constant success in protecting your information, network and systems assets 24×7.

Lawrence M. Oliva
Reston, Virginia
February 2004

Chapter I

Executive Overview

Lawrence M. Oliva

The Ubiquitous New World of IT Security

The convergence of many interdependent events, including the expansion of unprotected Internet connected applications, the global war on international terrorism and the large financial impacts of information and identity theft, has made IT security a core element of most corporate and government IT plans. During 2003, two examples illustrate the scope and cost of the security problem: Cyber attacks increased 40% in the first three quarters of the year, and the cost of cleaning up multiple worm and virus attacks during the summer cost $3.5 billion, according to the CERT Coordination Center, a cyber security-monitoring agency.

Interwoven with capacity, performance and reliability factors, internal security strategies have expanded past keeping external hackers and crackers out to authenticating users through biometric and other factors, tracking authorized access inside firewalls by system users, and forensic analysis of destructive software. Given the economic con-

Copyright © 2004, Idea Group Inc. Copying or distributing in print or electronic forms without written permission of Idea Group Inc. is prohibited.

straints placed on business expenses, however, these efforts have often been too little, too late to stop determined individuals from gaining access to information assets.

Adding to the technical complexity of security are legal issues concerning user privacy, liability issues for not preventing the theft of customer records and identities, and government compliance with HIPAA, GLBA, FCRA, NORPDA, PIPEDA, SAFETY, Sarbanes-Oxley, and the U.S. Patriot Act regulations. Overlaying proactive long-term plans and operations are immediate reactive limitation activities to network and system-wide attacks caused by malicious software (also called "malware") such as worms, viruses, Trojan horses and zombies.

As technology reliability has moved user expectations to a 24×7 availability level, the level of management complexity associated with that degree of service has required larger equipment investments, more staffing, and increased awareness of the consequences of each decision made concerning IT security. By default, IT managers and executives have been forced to become experts — with associated responsibilities — on many different topics outside the traditional IT community.

This added level of management complexity is just now being recognized in the IT community due to the pressure of meeting immediate production deadlines. Since September 11, 2001, passage of multiple legislation packages impacting the IT community, often indirectly, has occurred. The impact of these changes is still being determined by industry practitioners and the legal profession, with subsequent training activities required for full awareness and compliance by all affected groups. At a minimum, however, it is clear that security activities for information systems and assets will need to increase substantially to comply with these new regulations, or organizations will bear financial penalties and negligence legal determinations.

Copyright © 2004, Idea Group Inc. Copying or distributing in print or electronic forms without written permission of Idea Group Inc. is prohibited.

Security as a Process

IT security is no longer an "event" or part-time assignment for corporate and government organizations. It has become a continuous process every second of every day, from both the technology and management perspectives. Most executives of small companies are unaware that their corporate firewall is probed hundreds of times a day by automated attack tools. Financial services and government firewalls are often probed tens of thousands of times every day.

These attack tools — many are available for free through the Internet — can be deployed with a few mouse clicks against millions of systems. Once they find an unprotected or poorly protected system, the tools record IP (Internet Protocol) addresses and other information useful to hackers and crackers in exploiting the system or network for valuable data. Hackers may also turn the system into a denial-of-service (DoS) zombie to flood targeted systems with millions of messages and impair their ability to process and transmit legitimate information.

A strong security process contains several layers of operational functionality, including:

- External and internal access control points such as firewalls
- Strong user authentication for access and downloading
- Audit logging user network, system and information access
- Data encryption processes are applied where possible
- Using trusted partners for data exchange purposes
- Immediate installation of currently available software patches
- Training of internal and external users about password controls and unauthorized information access
- Physical security for equipment rooms, software backups and hardcopy documents

Copyright © 2004, Idea Group Inc. Copying or distributing in print or electronic forms without written permission of Idea Group Inc. is prohibited.

- Management policies for unauthorized usage, management monitoring and user privacy expectations
- A root cause analysis process for determining "what happened" when unexpected events occur
- A secure and comprehensive information and service recovery plan that can be immediately triggered should a disaster occur
- Management escalation chains so that small problems are contained quickly, and larger problems get resources assigned quickly

These layers build upon each other in redundant and incremental ways to create a fabric of security. For example, a strong authentication policy can prevent unknown users from gaining access to networks and systems. Known users can log in and perform their work with an audit trail about what they did and when they did it. Data are only accepted from trusted external sources to prevent contamination of databases with visibly corrupt — or worse, semi-valid — information.

The Value of Information Assets

Information has value to its owners, users, automated systems that must use it, and government agencies that regulate access to it. For example, Wal-Mart stores could not operate efficiently without a 30 terabyte data warehouse that tracks the cost, profit, shelf life, and other metrics associated with every product sold in every store during the past five years.

Major domestic and international airlines could not efficiently schedule and crew billions of dollars of equipment, nor operate their revenue capacity maximization models without the use of sophisticated databases and information systems valued over several billion dollars of replacement cost.

Copyright © 2004, Idea Group Inc. Copying or distributing in print or electronic forms without written permission of Idea Group Inc. is prohibited.

The business model for Visa, MasterCard International and American Express is based around card use data collection, account tracking, fraud analysis, customer billing and receipt collection information for hundreds of millions of credit and charge cards. The collective value of their databases and information assets is in the hundreds of billions of dollars — more than the annual budgets of all nations of the world, except for the U.S. and Japan.

Wall Street stock trading and financial institutions would not be able to open for business without having confidence in the accuracy of information used to conduct trades, base valuations on, or estimate earnings against. Accurate and trusted information is a core underpinning in market transparency and investor confidence.

Where does information derive its value? In part, from being able to infinitesimally leverage information for financial, operational, analytical, managerial, and social advantages. Once collected and verified as accurate, the value of information increases every time a successful transaction or usage occurs due to the cascade effect of each transaction triggering or enabling a second transaction and then a third, and so forth over time. The single transaction of selling 100 shares of stock, for example, may trigger purchases of other stock shares, purchases of capital goods such as automobiles, trucks, aircraft or property, which over time trigger purchases of other stock, maintenance and servicing of vehicles and property and employment of staff members. When viewed as a complete financial and transaction picture from beginning to end, accurate information enables transaction-based financial gain, marketing leverage, direct customer communications, and collaborative partnerships that would be prohibitively costly or complex to establish and support.

The concept that information has value was crystallized by Dr. David Nolan in his *Harvard Business Review* article in 1982 (Nolan, 1982) and revised by him and others since then. Recently, Nolan

Copyright © 2004, Idea Group Inc. Copying or distributing in print or electronic forms without written permission of Idea Group Inc. is prohibited.

(2001) has presented the concept that the value of information systems to organizations increases through a series of "stages" of technology evolution, from the mainframe era of 1960 to 1980, to the Micro era of 1980 to 1995, and the network (Internet) era of today. Inherent in the changes in technology is the ability to expand the use of information for beneficial and sometimes unforeseen purposes. Nolan reported that Microsoft used the Internet to distribute to, and communicate with, 400,000 beta customers of Windows 95 software. Responding to inputs received from these early users enabled Microsoft to redesign and redefine how the product worked prior to its final release to the market. Being able to use the Internet as a distribution system and customer communications vehicle, and linked to a integrated tracking systems permitted a beta test by hundreds of thousands of people — previous releases involved a small percentage of customers which did not provide a test environment as diverse as Windows 95 had.

While most executives and senior managers agree that information does indeed have value, they often calculate the value based on the cost to collect, maintain and manage it, rather than the potential value to be derived by the organization through leveraging the information to achieve business objectives and support their customer's needs, sometimes in ways previously unintended. For example, Gateway and Dell — initially manufacturers of personal computers — now use their massive customer databases to market plasma televisions, personal organizers, digital music players and other products not included in their original business models.

Since 1996, many e-gov initiatives have been aimed at leveraging and expanding the value of government provided and collected information. Many citizen-facing Web portals have been created by the U.S. Federal Government to provide access to tax refund information, contracting opportunities, park reservation information, transportation licensing and permits information, the status of pending legislation,

Copyright © 2004, Idea Group Inc. Copying or distributing in print or electronic forms without written permission of Idea Group Inc. is prohibited.

electronic sale and distribution of government publications, and many other purposes. Understanding that physical transactions can often be converted into electronic ones has leveraged government databases into 24×7 access points without the traditional overhead costs for staffing, physical space and communications systems.

Even small companies and organizations may have substantial value in their customer and partner information. Manufacturers and providers of unique goods and services can often leverage information on customer requirements or preferences into new business markets, similar to what Gateway and Dell have done. Information, once captured and validated for one purpose, can be combined with commercially available third-party databases to obtain historical trending and cross-product opportunities. For example, piano manufacturers may purchase a database from a manufacturer of high fidelity recording equipment to see if a customer might want to record their musical performances. Makers of batteries for digital cameras and cell phones are very interested in databases of customers from camera stores and cellular phone companies. Insurance companies that offer theft and damage protection polices for these products would also be interested in any of this information.

The concept of information having value is important to business and government. On a fundamental basis, if information has little (or no) value to the organization that owns or collects it, there is little reason to spend resources trying to protect it. Making a determination about the value of the organization's information is an incumbent responsibility for executive and senior management, as the decision drives multiple actions to either limit or permit access to information, systems and networks. Establishing the exact value of the information is not as important as determining if there is some — or great — value to be protected against loss, misuse or corruption.

Copyright © 2004, Idea Group Inc. Copying or distributing in print or electronic forms without written permission of Idea Group Inc. is prohibited.

Security Challenges and Responsibilities

With constantly increasing technical complexity, legal barriers and privacy expectations, the challenges of information security have risen exponentially in the past five years. The enormous drive in the late 1990s to Web-enable internal applications and drive market share often relegated security processes to a second or third level priority. When combined with continuing computer industry disagreement about the degree of user and access security standards, many financial and customer-facing systems that should be highly protected continue to use six-character passwords.

Opportunistic computer crime is now just a click or two away for just about anyone who can — and often does — download free hacking tools from the Internet. Information security engineers are familiar with how these tools work, and well-designed and maintained networks can usually block their penetration through the first level of firewalls. However, networks that are incorrectly configured, do not have current patches applied, or are not maintained — remember that security is a process, not a single event — are often successfully attacked, with information getting illegally obtained or destroyed.

Challenges faced by information technology support organizations include:

1. Knowing who should — and should not — have access to information, systems and networks. Accurate personnel records are sometimes not distributed quickly to the IT organization, or sometimes not kept at all, leading to a default access decision of "welcome".
2. Understanding the differences between a multitude of different, and sometimes conflicting, security technologies available from many unique suppliers.

Copyright © 2004, Idea Group Inc. Copying or distributing in print or electronic forms without written permission of Idea Group Inc. is prohibited.

3. Waiting for comprehensive security standards agreed upon by all major software and network suppliers and the federal government.
4. Maintaining a rapid response engineering capability to viruses, worms, Trojan horses, denial-of-service (DoS) attacks, as well as continuing network and access probing from hackers and crackers trying to gain access to valuable information.
5. Developing and maintaining accurate configuration management records concerning security software patch levels for critical and noncritical systems.
6. Knowing where to apply software patches for maximum impact to reduce user or production system impact — for example, gateway systems to public networks are usually the first line of defense, and should have the most current software levels compared to a system dedicated to printing bar code labels on the factory floor.
7. Providing the right level of access for employees and system users to do their jobs, without providing total access to all files and systems.
8. Knowing whom to trust for information transfers from suppliers, partners and customers. All information is not equal — e-mail attachments can contain worms and viruses, images can contain embedded messages (encryption known as steganography,) and executable files can contain trap doors and time bombs.
9. Attracting and retaining qualified information security engineers through educational and personal challenges.
10. Obtaining adequate budgets for equipment, personnel and service providers. Security is a cost of doing business, similar to keeping the lights on and telephones working.

Legal challenges continue to increase as attorneys begin to understand the technology components involved and the financial and

Copyright © 2004, Idea Group Inc. Copying or distributing in print or electronic forms without written permission of Idea Group Inc. is prohibited.

operational impact of losing valuable information to unauthorized users. Technology developers, suppliers and service providers are increasingly being blamed for not designing secure software or systems, and not planning for all possible security scenarios. IT management is being challenged and blamed for not doing everything possible to employ the best defenses against unauthorized access or information loss. Users are being blamed for carelessly losing or sharing passwords, security access tokens, and user IDs, often against company or organization policy. Of course, hackers — when found and identified — are arrested and jailed.

As larger and larger value computer crimes occur, more and more blame is being distributed to IT executive and senior management, often with the connotation that "they should have known this could have happened". Given the global trends concerning information and identity theft, it is clear that IT management should plan for worst case scenarios, although they may be infrequent in number.

However, IT executive and senior management must retain a vigilant posture concerning information security, as the impact of a successful attack or theft can be devastating to customers and the organization in terms of loss of customer trust, unreliable information and corrective action expenses.

Internet-related fraud accounted for more than 55% of more than 500,000 consumer complaints filed with the Federal Trade Commission in 2003, according to the agency, up 45% from 2002. The agency reports the median loss for victims of Internet-related fraud was $195. Identity theft was the most common complaint for the fourth consecutive year, representing 42% of all complaints in 2003 (FTC, 2004.)

Unfortunately, the information technology executive team's responsibilities related to safeguarding corporate, citizen, and personal information continue to expand through legislation, market force expectations and court ordered restitution. For example, since 1996

Copyright © 2004, Idea Group Inc. Copying or distributing in print or electronic forms without written permission of Idea Group Inc. is prohibited.

Congress has passed several regulations including HIPAA, GLBA, 21 C.F.R. Part 11 (FDA drug manufacture), Sarbanes-Oxley and E-SIGN that specify how information must be protected from unauthorized users and purposes, and/or provide for transparency and verification of trusted information.

In 2003 the "Do Not Call" list went into effect, blocking telemarketing calls for most private businesses not having an existing customer relationship. Anti-telemarketing forces prevailed on Congress to overcome the last minute legal challenges to the law. Privacy advocates, such as the Electronic Frontier Association and the National Law Center, are actively monitoring identify theft events and responses by business to force innovative approaches to stop theft of private information and assist the victims of this crime. These privacy advocates and others are equally alarmed by the proposed use of the airline passenger screening program named "CAPPS2", which profiles every passenger's identity using a combination of private and public databases. Government sources have stated that passenger information in the CAPPS database will be deleted a few days after a trip has been completed, but privacy advocates have not been provided details. Airline passengers have started to independently pursue litigation against the airlines' sharing of their personal data, but it is not clear what, if any, viable alternatives to this screening process airline transportation travelers have.

From the IT perspective, it is probable that businesses and government organizations will be asked to provide confidential business and customer information to be used for security screening purposes. It is probable that customers and partners will be very displeased with this situation, and will try to apply market force pressures — boycotting companies that provide the information, filing litigation, and providing incomplete information — to stop its proliferation and enforcement. Complying with these mandates will increase

Copyright © 2004, Idea Group Inc. Copying or distributing in print or electronic forms without written permission of Idea Group Inc. is prohibited.

operational costs for IT organizations, and escalate the financial and legal exposure for noncompliance.

Courts have begun to order restitution in cases of egregious business error in personal privacy cases such as massive credit card theft from poorly protected business databases, medical records stolen from hospital files, and allowing obvious identity theft to continue after customer notification to the originating organization. IT executive and senior managers need to be aware of these legal challenges and expectations during strategic technology and investment planning so that changes can be incorporated into existing processes and systems with minimal cost instead of being added at the last minute at great expense.

Copyright © 2004, Idea Group Inc. Copying or distributing in print or electronic forms without written permission of Idea Group Inc. is prohibited.

Section I

Governance Issues

Balancing Access with Control

How does management determine who should have access to some information and not have access to other information? Would giving everyone access to all information mean a total loss of management control? How can control be managed when customers want to have direct access to their information 24×7 through public portals?

This section examines several key areas of focus critical to balancing access with control mechanisms. First is a detailed chapter on aligning security, countermeasures and business process — elements that require substantial senior management decisions and direction on, as they form the framework for the overall IT architecture and technology purchased to support it.

Next comes a detailed discussion about protecting customer provided information — a key element in every information security plan. The next major chapter focuses on multiple aspects of risk management, specifically people, processes, technology and the hierarchy of controls.

Toward the end of the section are discussions on the costs and benefits of IT security programs, trusting trusted systems, and best practices for sharing data outside the organization.

Copyright © 2004, Idea Group Inc. Copying or distributing in print or electronic forms without written permission of Idea Group Inc. is prohibited.

Chapter II

Aligning Assurance Requirements, Countermeasures, and Business

Craig E. Kaucher
National Defense University, USA

Introduction

The latest year-end statistics from the highly regarded CERT Coordination Center (CERT-CC) at Carnegie Mellon University once again demonstrate that there is little evidence of improvement in information assurance. The number of incidents reported to CERT-CC once again nearly doubled from the previous year, and for the first time exceeded the six-figure mark at 137,529 for 2003 (CERT, 2004).

Various surveys of the business community put the cost of information security breaches in the billions of dollars. One survey by security company Trend Micro put the cost of computer viruses alone at $55 billion worldwide in 2003 (Reuters, 2004). Another survey of

Copyright © 2004, Idea Group Inc. Copying or distributing in print or electronic forms without written permission of Idea Group Inc. is prohibited.

government and corporate leaders from around the world by PriceWaterhouseCoopers and CIO Magazine stated that their top priority for 2004 would be to raise end-user awareness (CIO, 2003), which may indicate that emphasis across organizations, and from the top to the bottom, is still lacking.

Governmental organizations also continue to struggle with securing their information. Federal government agencies in particular continue to be cited for weak information security. A January 2003 report by the General Accounting Office (GAO) found that many agencies of the federal government had noted "increased management attention to and accountability for information security" since the enactment of the Government Information Security Reform Act in 2001, but "Although improvements are underway, recent audits of 24 of the largest federal agencies continue to identify significant information security weaknesses that put critical federal operations and assets in each of these agencies at risk" (GAO, 2004). This report specifically identified security program management and access control as the two most often identified weaknesses. In fact, security program management, defined by the GAO as "the framework for ensuring that risks are understood and that effective controls are selected and properly implemented" was the only area in which every one of the 24 major federal agencies audited was found to have weaknesses. This statistic was also unchanged from another GAO audit one year earlier.

Why is it that security program management remains a weakness across nearly every federal agency, and why is this concern also mirrored in the corporate world? One might wonder also how awareness can still remain a top concern, when the prevalence and impact of incidents is so widely reported. What are the hurdles that both government and industry face in institutionalizing information assurance and security in information-age organizations?

Copyright © 2004, Idea Group Inc. Copying or distributing in print or electronic forms without written permission of Idea Group Inc. is prohibited.

When many people hear the terms *information assurance* or *security,* they tend to think in terms of problems. Certainly, the mention of information assurance or security to many people today immediately reminds them of the problems that they personally or their organizations have suffered through with the latest rounds of malware. Others, sometimes in organizations that handle more sensitive or classified information, may immediately think of their perceived biggest problem, the insider threat.

More technically oriented individuals may say with a lot of conviction that the problem lies mainly in the widespread use and distribution of software that is inherently insecure. People who read a lot of popular publications and news stories may say that the big problem in information assurance today is anything wireless.

Blaming so-called "hackers" is so common that it is almost passé. And people who like to show us all that they are really big, strategic thinkers, looking boldly into their crystal balls to predict the future, may say that a new form of terror, cyber terrorism, is now upon us, and so this is a big, big problem.

This approach to information assurance is very reactive, at best, and quite possibly totally ineffective at the worst. In fact, it may be the antithesis of effective information assurance. Because labeling things that are in reality a few, among many, many possible threats to your information and information systems, or a few among many, many possible vulnerabilities within your information and information systems as "the problem" automatically excludes the context of the situation, ignores the information assurance requirements for that given situation, and will probably result in a patchwork approach to mitigating any future risk to your organization.

So if we delve a little deeper into the "problems" we may begin to ask some questions such as these. Have we done all that we could to

Copyright © 2004, Idea Group Inc. Copying or distributing in print or electronic forms without written permission of Idea Group Inc. is prohibited.

cover all potential avenues by which viruses, worms, and other malware could be introduced into our environment?

What do we do to determine whether a potential new hire, or a long time employee could possibly be a malicious inside threat? And also, what are we doing on an ongoing basis to mitigate the non-malicious insider?

Do we really need to make our organization part of a global beta-test of the latest version of "Server Software X" before we have some assurance of its security and stability?

A few years ago, information security people worried about the "rogue modem" that provided a back-door into the information infrastructure. Now the problem with wireless capabilities may be much bigger, because while the rogue modem probably serviced only one user at that particular workstation, the rogue Wireless Access Point in the wrong place could provide back-door access to an unknown number of potential threats.

We may also believe that "the sys admins" or "the network guys" are taking care of our information assurance needs ... Oh by the way, wasn't that just outsourced?

And who would possibly want to attack poor, little old me, just sitting here on my office PC, minding my own business, just doing my job, which shouldn't threaten anybody?

So one step away from what are often perceived and described as our information assurance "problems", we find a collection of behaviors, roles and responsibilities, and beliefs, that all belong to ... somebody! And they are not all from just one part of the organization. They may very well be the entire organization!

We are constantly in contact with information and information systems, at home, at work, and at nearly every point and instance in between. We may be almost becoming oblivious to our constant use of information and interaction with systems.

Copyright © 2004, Idea Group Inc. Copying or distributing in print or electronic forms without written permission of Idea Group Inc. is prohibited.

We do have a variety of needs, professionally, personally, and in mixed contexts, to assure the information. When we move through and in between our business and personal lives, these assurance requirements may change.

The means of assuring information are growing in quantity, and hopefully quality, but are they growing fast enough? And do we recognize and effectively employ all the means necessary to meet the requirements?

The real problem in information assurance is that today, we may fail to realize the full context in which information present in, and used by our organization exists. We may have a lack of understanding of what the information assurance requirements are, and we may not know what the means, and roles and responsibilities to meet these requirements for information assurance are.

At the corporate, or strategic, or executive level, as a minimum level of awareness, an executive or senior manager needs to understand the relationship between these three things: context, requirements, and means. Understanding each of these as well as the relationship between them can come at the intersection of information assurance and enterprise architecture.

This chapter will focus on bringing together three emerging trends, information assurance requirements, enterprise architecture, and defense-in-depth, which in a coordinated fashion can form a framework that will provide a common understanding of information assurance requirements for specific architectural contexts, as well as the assignment of effective risk-mitigating approaches. It is vital to establish and understand the relationship between these three trends, information assurance requirements, enterprise architecture, and defense in depth measures. Understanding this relationship will enable organizations in both the corporate world and in government to maximize the effectiveness of their information assurance programs.

Copyright © 2004, Idea Group Inc. Copying or distributing in print or electronic forms without written permission of Idea Group Inc. is prohibited.

What Do We Want ?

The first step in building an effective information assurance program is to understand exactly what we want when we desire "security" or "assurance". What is the specific effect that we want to achieve?

Think about building a house. A requirement that nearly everyone may have when building a house is for it to be safe and secure. Would it be sufficient to just say to your builder, "Build me a safe and secure house" and then to expect to get exactly what you wanted? "Safe and secure" could be interpreted in many different ways, depending on what role one plays in the building effort.

What would "safe and secure" mean to the parents of several young children? Would "childproof" be more accurate? On the other end of the chronological spectrum, "safe and secure" to an elderly, retired couple may mean an entirely different home design.

Depending on the environment where the home was being built, "safe and secure" could have some different meanings also. There could be special structural requirements due to the frequency of hurricanes, tornados, or even earthquakes in the area. Perhaps high temperatures or an abundance of snowfall could become factors in determining what "safe and secure" really means.

Of course, "fireproof" could also be a specific example of "safe and secure" as well. And finally, the prospective homeowners could simply be concerned with physical security.

But beyond just the homeowners' desires for a safe and secure home, there may also be other parties with the same or different interests in the meaning of "safe and secure". In all likelihood, the homeowners will have a mortgage, and in order to get the mortgage, another party will have to be involved as well: an insurance company to provide homeowners' insurance. In order to get the loan, the homeowners will need that insurance policy, and in order to get the

Copyright © 2004, Idea Group Inc. Copying or distributing in print or electronic forms without written permission of Idea Group Inc. is prohibited.

policy, or to be able to afford it, the homeowners will need to convince the insurance company that the home is worth insuring. An insurance company will not want to offer a policy on the proverbial "house of straw", preferring instead that the homeowner build with something stronger and somewhat less combustible.

The homeowner, builder, and others such as the bank and insurance company, may also have to pay attention to governmental standards for "safe and secure" homes, in the form of zoning regulations and building codes. In fact, there may even be penalties and incentives regarding complicance with the codes and regulations: fines from the local municipality for failing to follow zoning laws, and lower insurance premiums for safety features above and beyond the minimal requirements. In some areas, there may also be applicable requirements imposed by a homeowners' association. Though such associations usually do not need to develop detailed codes or bylaws for physical or structural safety and security, they can contribute to complicance by requiring major home additions to be completed under a building permit issued by the local government, and they can also contribute to safety through efforts such as a neighborhood watch program.

So depending on your perspective, safe and secure can have a number of different or more specific meanings. All of the many different perspectives may be equally valid and need to be met. And all of the different views must be understood by the homeowner.

So What is an Information Assurance Requirement?

In attempting to assure their information, government organizations have struggled with having all those involved with this effort on the same page in understanding the real requirement. The first component

Copyright © 2004, Idea Group Inc. Copying or distributing in print or electronic forms without written permission of Idea Group Inc. is prohibited.

that we need to understand is our requirements for information assurance.

Five items, confidentiality, integrity, availability, non-repudiation, and authentication, have become the somewhat "traditional" list of requirements. They are listed and defined in both DOD and other federal government documents, such as the National Information Assurance Glossary, published by the Committee on National Security Systems (CNSS) as Instruction Number 4009 (NSTISSC, 2004). But they may not be all-inclusive of assurance requirements for all contexts in every organization.

The ISO security architecture reference model (ISO 7498-2) (ISO, 2004), for example, lists seven layers, reflecting a high level view of the different requirements within network security, adding access control and notarization/signature to the traditional elements.

In a research note for the Gartner Group, Roberta Witty describes and defines several requirements in addition to the traditional five, including authorization, privacy, and noninterference (Witty, 2002).

Gurpreet Dhillon and James Backhouse also affirm some of the traditional requirements, while suggesting three additional principles contained in what they call RITE, which include responsibility, integrity, trust, and ethicality (Dhillon, 2000).

An even more expansive listing of potential requirements may include what Holmes Miller describes as the "10 dimensions of information quality", which include relevance, accuracy, timeliness, completeness, coherence, format, accessibility, compatibility, security, and validity (Holmes, 1996).

And finally, in addition to several of the potential requirements already listed, IBM researchers Anbazhagen Mani and Arun Nagarajan add to their list of "major requirements for supporting Quality of Service services" the regulatory requirement (Mani, 2003).

Copyright © 2004, Idea Group Inc. Copying or distributing in print or electronic forms without written permission of Idea Group Inc. is prohibited.

Which list do you follow? Some may argue that some terms are inherently contained within the definition of others non-repudiation and authentication as parts of confidentiality, for example. Others argue for rolling the set of requirements back to circa 1991, when John McCumber described confidentiality, integrity and availability as the information characteristics of his INFOSEC model (McCumber, 1991). But such arguments miss the point.

The rationale for defining requirements for information assurance with as much specificity as possible is to permit later the application of the most effective means of meeting those requirements. Generalization of requirements through an overly restrictive set of options may lead to unintended consequences. Generalization may increase the chance that incorrect or ineffective countermeasures or means of attaining assurance are applied, and that the specific intended assurance outcome is not attained. Generalization may also cause an organization to be ignorant of new and emerging requirements.

For example, take an assurance requirement for privacy. The new Health Insurance Portability and Accountability Act of 1996 (HIPAA) was enacted to protect the privacy of patients' health and medical information. According to the U.S. Department of Health and Human Services, "The regulations protect medical records and other individually identifiable health information, whether it is on paper, in computers or communicated orally". HIPAA, in fact, includes a "privacy rule" that describes specific instances in which confidentiality, integrity, and availability should be considered. There are also many instances in which health information may be disclosed (U.S. Dept. of Health and Human Services, 2003). In this case the requirement, privacy, is not narrower than just confidentiality, for example, but includes other elements of the "traditional" list as well. Simply viewing privacy as synonymous with confidentiality would be incorrect, and applying only

Copyright © 2004, Idea Group Inc. Copying or distributing in print or electronic forms without written permission of Idea Group Inc. is prohibited.

countermeasures to protect against threats to confidentiality would be inadequate to meet the requirement for privacy.

If understanding the true information assurance requirement is the first step to providing effective information assurance, then an open mind to consideration of the nature of the specific requirement is necessary. Standard definitions may be useful for an academic understanding of requirements, but they should not be used to drive operational situations where real, specific assurance requirements must be met. Each organization that has a need for effective information assurance must first decide what their real requirement is, and must then ensure that the requirement is well understood throughout the organization.

Defending Information in Depth ... in All Directions

Many organizations are coming to realize that information assurance involves more than just securing information technology systems with more technology. Information assurance also involves a shared responsibility among everyone in an organization.

The "defense in depth" approach to information assurance was first popularized by the Department of Defense, and involves applying technological, operational, and people-related countermeasures to mitigate information assurance risks in a holistic manner (Joint Chiefs of Staff, 2003). People-oriented actions may include such things as training and personnel security. Operational actions such as plans, policies, and guidelines are also a part of the strategy, and technology activities such as system redundancy, intrusion detection, and firewalls may also be employed.

Copyright © 2004, Idea Group Inc. Copying or distributing in print or electronic forms without written permission of Idea Group Inc. is prohibited.

These three prongs of defense in depth could arguably include almost any imaginable means of assuring information and mitigating risks to it. Most if not all sub-elements of these three capabilities also arguably involve in some respect the other two capabilities as well.

Consider, for example, an intrusion detection system (IDS). Generally an IDS system is thought of as a technology in the form of a network or host-based IDS. The technology is designed to detect unauthorized or anomalous activities on the system or network. But just like the earlier example of the home security IDS, at the point where a legitimate incident is detected, a person will be notified, and become involved. The person, whether monitoring a home or a network, ought to be following an established operational procedure that governs further investigation and reporting on the incident. If the person responsible for doing the monitoring is poorly trained, despite the great capabilities of the technology, at a minimum an unauthorized intrusion may take place, and at the worst, whether in the home or on the network, a catastrophe may occur. Likewise, a weak policy or poorly written procedure can render technological effectiveness a moot point.

So once again, as with generalization of requirements, simple categorization of the elements of defense in depth as technology, people, or operations, is perhaps inadequate. A more careful consideration of the necessary interrelationships and dependencies between the elements of the defense in depth strategy is required in order to employ these countermeasures effectively.

Broadly considered, defense in depth can also have a "force multiplier" effect by actively involving more parts of an organization, and thus more people, in assuring information. When more means or countermeasures are employed, more roles in defense in depth are established, and when managed well, the effectiveness of the strategy is enhanced.

Copyright © 2004, Idea Group Inc. Copying or distributing in print or electronic forms without written permission of Idea Group Inc. is prohibited.

Several other lists of means provide more defined elements that can be part of a defense in depth strategy. ISO Standard 17799, for example, includes compliance, security organization, and asset classification and control, among its list of 10 elements (ISO, 2000).

Internet Security Systems describes a security management lifecycle, centered on security policy, standards, and guidelines, and consisting of the steps of assess, design, deploy, manage and support, surrounded by ongoing education (Internet Security Systems, 2000).

Electronic Data Systems also describes an information assurance lifecycle consisting of the steps of assess, protect, validate, train, and monitor (EDS, 2000).

Regardless of whether we consider all of the means as a concept, or process, or lifecycle, or in any other form, it is most important that we recognize that they are much more than the technologies that many people think of when they hear the term *information assurance,* and they therefore will involve many more people within an organization in the overall information assurance effort.

The Architect

Our homeowners have discovered that they and others have a variety of requirements that need to be addressed in order to establish a safe and secure home. Just as the requirements came from a number of sources, so too do the means of meeting them.

In order to protect themselves and their children, the physical structure of the home, the environment in which the home will be built, and also their financial security, they will have to employ an array of means. Some will involve approved products, best practices, and closely supervised installation and configuration. Other means will

Copyright © 2004, Idea Group Inc. Copying or distributing in print or electronic forms without written permission of Idea Group Inc. is prohibited.

involve well understood and enforced policy, and monitoring services. While the house is under construction, carpenters, plumbers, electricians, roofers, and their suppliers and supervisors will be involved. A series of inspectors will verify compliance with building codes, and plans. Systems will be tested. And before the home is finally occupied, a final certification will need to be granted.

So who will ensure that all requirements are addressed, and that all means are effectively employed, and that everything fits and works together? Our requirements and the means selected to meet them must meet in a common context. This context is called an architecture.

The architect will create a series of documentation that portrays a variety of perspectives of the home. People with different skills in providing each of the means will each use a portion of the documents produced by the architect to fit their means into the overall context of the home. The documents for the carpenters, for example, will only show those aspects of construction that are relevant to carpentry.

The architect will be the central controller of all of these different perspectives. If changes need to be made in one discipline, electrical wiring for example, the architect will make sure that the change does not adversely impact any other aspect of the home.

Well done architectural documentation will not only serve a purpose during construction of the home. If the homeowners are able to retain a set of the architectural drawings, then they will be able to refer to them throughout their ownership of the home whenever they want to plan a modification to the home. The homeowners could choose to annotate, or maintain the architectural documents so that they have a current, accurate depiction of the relationship of the various components of the home.

Copyright © 2004, Idea Group Inc. Copying or distributing in print or electronic forms without written permission of Idea Group Inc. is prohibited.

Enterprise Architecture: The Evolution of an Opportunity

Information assurance and enterprise architecture are not new concepts or programs. In fact, for those in the federal government, they are both mandated activities, with requirements and reporting detailed in various policies, regulations, and laws. Increasingly in the corporate world as well, through legislation such as HIPAA in the health services sector, Sarbanes-Oxley Act for public accounting and audit firms, and the Gramm-Leach-Bliley Act for financial services companies, information assurance programs are becoming a requirement. There are no legal or regulatory mandates for enterprise architecture in the private sector, although many companies choose to adopt some form of it as a best practice.

Why is enterprise architecture used in government? Federal agencies are being called upon to account for their information technology spending, and to demonstrate how their information technology systems are supporting the accomplishment of their mission. Enterprise architecture efforts are involving more than just the information technologists of an organization. In fact, initial government-wide steps taken to define the federal enterprise architecture involve establishing a business reference model, to be followed later by data and technical reference models.

Enterprise architecture programs in both the civilian agencies of the federal government, as well as in the Department of Defense provide a variety of perspectives, linking business, operational, and technical views of a mission or process. Just as the home architect provides each specialist with his or her own perspective, the government architectures provide a centrally controlled, related set of views. Managers can see an operational prespective, while information technology specialists can see technical views.

Copyright © 2004, Idea Group Inc. Copying or distributing in print or electronic forms without written permission of Idea Group Inc. is prohibited.

In the past, there has been very little reference to, or integration of information assurance into enterprise architecture, even in the federal government where both programs are mandated activities. That is beginning to change as a broader acceptance of the importance of information assurance spreads throughout federal agencies, and references to elements of information assurance are beginning to appear in the latest editions of the federal enterprise architecture framework.

It does not matter whether you take an approach such as the Federal Enterprise Architecture Framework, or the DOD Architecture Framework, or any other approach that an organization adopts and maintains that holistically includes business and operational, as well as technical elements.

Some may also suggest some modification of the Zachman framework, although both of these approaches are strongly rooted in information technology architecture, and may be somewhat limited when attempting to describe the total context in which information may have to be assured (Zachman, 2001).

A holistic approach is preferred because we want our context to focus on information, and not just information systems or technology. We want ultimately to determine our requirements for information assurance, not IS or IT assurance. It is the loss of information, not any system or technology that we are trying to prevent, and assuring information as opposed to systems or technology is an entirely different problem (Von Solms, 2001).

Requirements, Means, and Architectures all Meet

While understanding information assurance requirements, the means or countermeasures to meet the requirements, and the context or

Copyright © 2004, Idea Group Inc. Copying or distributing in print or electronic forms without written permission of Idea Group Inc. is prohibited.

Figure 1.

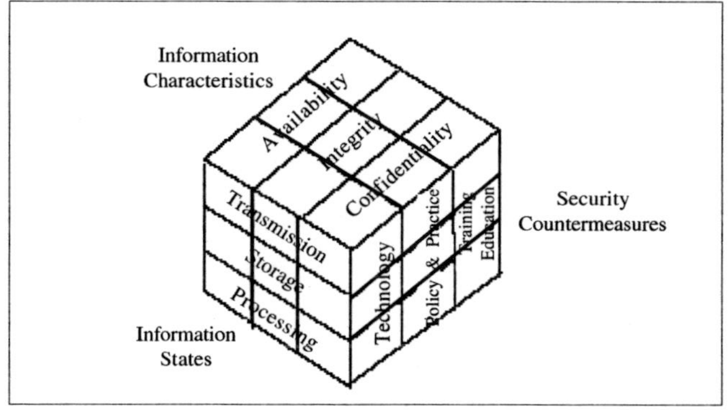

architecture to which they are applied is important, it is equally important to understand how these three things are related. Understanding such a complex set of relationships can be a daunting task. Fortunately, there are a series of models that can help to explain how requirements means and architectures are related.

In 1991, a young Air Force officer, Captain John McCumber proposed what he called a "comprehensive model" of information security, depicted in Figure 1 (McCumber, 1991).

What we have been calling *information assurance requirements* were referred to by McCumber as *information characteristics.* McCumber referred only to confidentiality, availability, and integrity.

What we call today *defense in depth,* McCumber called *security countermeasures.* People, operations, and technology have replaced McCumber's three components of security countermeasures, technology, policy and practice, and training and education in defense in depth.

The third side of McCumber's model was what he called *information states.* McCumber said that all information exists in one of three states: transmission, processing, or storage. McCumber allows that information can occasionally exist in two of the three states at one time.

Copyright © 2004, Idea Group Inc. Copying or distributing in print or electronic forms without written permission of Idea Group Inc. is prohibited.

For example, in a message system, the message could, while in transmission, also be in storage.

In 2001, Maconachy et al. described how “INFOSEC has evolved into Information Assurance (IA). This is more than a simple semantic change” (Maconachy et al., 2001)[1] The authors of this new model proposed a number of changes to update McCumber’s model. The elements that McCumber called *information characteristics* were referred to by the authors as *security services,* and were expanded to include authentication and non-repudiation. The 2001 model also updated McCumber’s security countermeasures to the current defense in depth trio of people, operations, and technology. The third side of McCumber’s model, information states, was left unchanged. The authors did suggest that a fourth dimension, time, ought also to be considered in several ways. The 2001 model, including a depiction of the time dimension, is depicted in Figure 2.

Today, with the emergence of comprehensive enterprise architecture frameworks, organizations have the opportunity to leverage the holistic approach of enterprise architecture to achieve a more advanced integration of information assurance requirements and countermea-

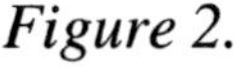
Figure 2.

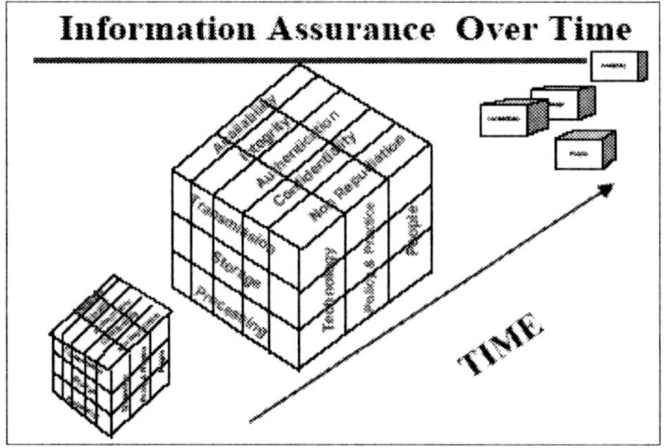

Copyright © 2004, Idea Group Inc. Copying or distributing in print or electronic forms without written permission of Idea Group Inc. is prohibited.

sures with the way information is used in an organization than ever before. This opportunity can be conceptually portrayed through a further advancement to the 2001 version of the McCumber model.

While the 2001 version by Maconachy et al. advanced McCumber's three information characteristics to five security states, and updated his security countermeasures to reflect the current defense in depth approach, the transmission, processing, and storage paradigm of information states was left unchanged.

McCumber's intent in describing information states may be viewed as an approach to allow a snapshot analysis of the relationship of information at any point in time within a system to security and countermeasures. His conceptual model has proven to be highly useful for educating information security professionals. At the time it was first conceived, with computer networks and information systems in a state of relative infancy, and true enterprise architecture a distant dream, McCumber's information states were a "good enough" approach to describing this third dimension of the cube.

Enterprise architecture, as a replacement to McCumber's information states, allows for an unprecedented level of fidelity and understanding of information assurance requirements and countermeasures as they relate to how information is used in the organization. Using enterprise architecture as the third dimension affords an organization the ability to examine information assurance requirements with respect to business processes, operational procedures, and technological infrastructure in an integrated and coordinated fashion. This enhancement of McCumber's model, and the update by Maconachy et al., is depicted in Figure 3.

There are a variety of advantages to be gained by this new approach. Using enterprise architecture provides a mission-technology linkage to which information assurance requirements and countermeasures can be applied. Enterprise architecture also provides a business

Copyright © 2004, Idea Group Inc. Copying or distributing in print or electronic forms without written permission of Idea Group Inc. is prohibited.

Figure 3.

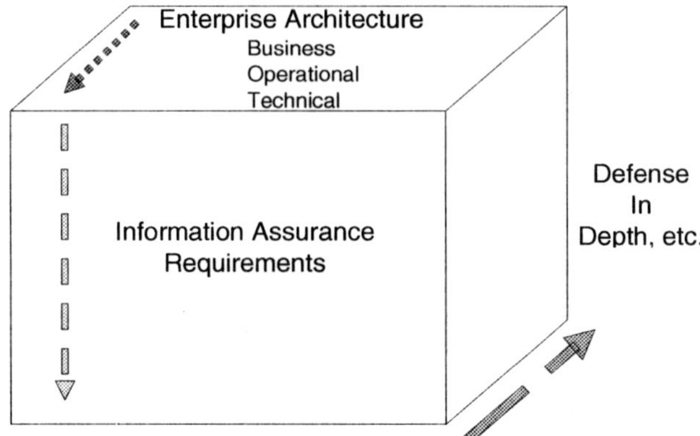

information-driven approach, as opposed to the earlier models that were systems-oriented.

As all enterprise architectures begin with the mission of the organization, this new model therefore inherently involves top-level leaders, who define the organization's mission.

When the fidelity of enterprise architecture, rather than the earlier information states, is applied to the third dimension of the model, information is portrayed in a much more relevant context.

Enterprise architecture, viewed in relation to information assurance requirements and countermeasures, also creates visibility of role-based perspectives of requirements and defense in depth. Anyone looking at their architectural perspective, whether business process, operations, or technically oriented, should be able to see the corresponding information assurance requirements and countermeasures for that portion of the architecture.

In this way also, senior leaders can be given the opportunity to decide at an enterprise level which information assurance requirements are suitable across the organization. All members of the organization

Copyright © 2004, Idea Group Inc. Copying or distributing in print or electronic forms without written permission of Idea Group Inc. is prohibited.

will be afforded the opportunity to participate in defining what necessary information assurance requirements and countermeasures there are for the specific elements of the enterprise architecture with which they are concerned. Everyone in the organization also has their context-appropriate understanding of their role in information assurance.

Conclusions

Despite rapid advances in technology, innovative policy and procedural approaches, and an ever-increasing emphasis on education, training and awareness, information assurance is not becoming any easier to do well. A new conceptual approach that considers requirements for information assurance in greater specificity, is inclusive of all possible means of defense, and recognizes how information, rather than systems, is used to support an organization's business processes is needed.

This third generation McCumber model, with the addition of enterprise architecture, is largely conceptual, but can form the basis of an analytical and engineering approach to matching requirements and countermeasures with information. This approach merges the disciplines of information assurance and management as never before, and provides a framework that can be continuously evolved.

As technology, business processes, and the threats to them continue to change, security must not just attempt to keep pace, but must seek opportunities to move out in front and stay ahead. "Build it in, don't add it on later" has been the mantra of security specialists for years. But good building does not start with all the tradesmen gathering at the construction site. A good building starts with a plan. The plan is architecture. And that is where security should also start.

Copyright © 2004, Idea Group Inc. Copying or distributing in print or electronic forms without written permission of Idea Group Inc. is prohibited.

Employee Monitoring and Privacy

In most cases, commercial and government organizations are able to monitor employee usage of company owned or provided equipment and networks. A formal policy document for employee distribution stating the organization permits (or does not permit) specific uses of the equipment provides guidelines. Along with a statement that the employee should not expect any privacy in their use of the system is often all that is needed for enforcement of the policy.

But, where should the line be drawn for acceptable personal use? Excluding the obvious list of gambling, pornographic, illegal pharmaceuticals and on-line commerce sites, what is reasonable? During winter months, does it make sense to permit employees to check the weather.com Web site to determine how powerful an imminent storm is? What about allowing parents to visit a daycare Web site that has Webcams installed to check on their children? What about checking CNN.com for news when a major disaster or accident strikes close to home that could harm their families or themselves during a commute home?

A management decision that applies common sense to what is and is not acceptable would seem to be the best approach to take, as it is impossible to specify every possible situation that could occur. What is important — from both the employee and employer perspectives — is that a written policy containing the guidelines be sent to all employees so that they are aware of it. As technology continues to make progress, and new and clever products and services are available for use, will there be exceptions for management to consider? Of course — right now, instant messaging devices (IM) and camera-enabled phones are two new areas of concern for information security and privacy. Policies should be developed (or expanded) for both of these technologies to

Copyright © 2004, Idea Group Inc. Copying or distributing in print or electronic forms without written permission of Idea Group Inc. is prohibited.

reflect management's expectations of their use (or non-use) in the workplace.

Many organizations that employ customer service agents monitor and record telephone calls and e-mails to ensure consistent customer service and delivery quality. Employees working these positions should know of corporate policies and standards about recording their conversations and messages through multiple messages, as well as from their supervisors. From an information security perspective, telling customers too much information may be just as damaging as telling them too little; for example, in the case of medical insurance claim processing or routine medical laboratory results.

In some cases — such as in the financial securities markets and with police and military agencies — it may make sense to create and maintain a security audit logfile for every transaction that occurs when a user logs in, accesses information, or sends files out of the system. Obviously, such a tracking capability is very expensive to build and support, but should a security breech occur, it does provide information useful in understanding what happened, when and by whom. All of these details are critical in making a determination about the severity of the security breech, collateral damage, and what must be done to limit further impact to the organization, its people, its customers and its shareholders.

Administrative Security Policies

Administrative security policies apply to the system administration activities such as entering user names and security privileges. A small team of highly trusted and experienced system or security engineers who have been given access to the superuser or sys admin passwords and accounts typically performs these functions. In almost all situations they follow detailed processes and policies to add people, remove

Copyright © 2004, Idea Group Inc. Copying or distributing in print or electronic forms without written permission of Idea Group Inc. is prohibited.

people and change their approved access levels. These processes provide consistency and auditability to both the admin and user in case of technical errors or security breeches.

From an IT management perspective, there are two critical elements of control: (a) Having trusted administrators who possess significant technical expertise, and (b) Developing and maintaining comprehensive administrative security policies that align with the needs of the business. Many organizations focus on the first element, and assume that the second element will be taken care of by the system administrator. In some cases, this does occur, but in many cases system administrators do not have the training to write a security policy that aligns with, and stays current to, the organization's business objectives.

Given that the majority of security problems are internal to the organization, it is incumbent upon management to review system administration policies and procedures at least once a year to ensure required security levels are being followed. Obtaining a third party audit and certification of the processes is also a prudent approach. Specific items to note in administrative security policies include:

- Defining multiple approval levels for adding new people to the system (this prevents a single point of failure)
- Frequently reviewing security access levels and privileges to provide higher or lower levels of user access
- Rotating staff members with security granting permissions into new and different assignments every few months to reduce the opportunity for a long term security breach with little fear of being caught
- Having a formal process for tracking and filing paper documents that detail when a user was added to the system and when changes occurred to their access level
- Having a security audit function to review paperwork and process compliance

Copyright © 2004, Idea Group Inc. Copying or distributing in print or electronic forms without written permission of Idea Group Inc. is prohibited.

- Avoiding known "conflicts of interest" between security admins and users, such as a husband approving his wife for a high level access. Have a neutral third party perform system administration work for known conflicts of interest access to the system
- Ensuring that system security admins have current training on all aspects of the specific technology they are responsible for supporting in addition to the organization's policies and procedures
- Linking security policies to business policies protecting the business from internal and external attacks while maximizing customer and supplier access to information they need to purchase products and services or replenish inventories

Professional Accountability

Shareholder Communications in Crisis and Non-Crisis Situations

Every organization has shareholders or stakeholders involved with, or having a stake in, its operations, procedures and ultimate financial or citizen-facing results. As information technology is used in almost every business environment, shareholders are aware of the benefits and risks, and want to be kept current about good news and bad news. When operations are going well with few and normal problems, routine reports and e-mail updates every week or two is a reasonable frequency. However, should an information security breach occur causing organizational financial or legal exposure, shareholders require a very high level of communications with and between executives and senior management. The IT organization needs to establish four dimensions of communications:

1. Identifying shareholder and customer expectations
2. Establishing direct communication channels

Copyright © 2004, Idea Group Inc. Copying or distributing in print or electronic forms without written permission of Idea Group Inc. is prohibited.

3. Developing the message
4. Managing the message

IT executives and senior managers have the same problem as elected politicians: cutting through the "noise" to answer questions and provide information. In today's 24-hour news cycle environment, almost anything occurring in the world can turn good news cold, and bad news hot. It is a fact of life that shareholders and customers collect and review information on a 24x7 basis and compare the media provided information against management reports to understand the differences, if any. During times of crisis such as a major security breach, accidental release of customer files or information, loss of data during a storm, or the inability to handle high volumes of sales data, the volume of information impedes "understanding" exactly what is happening or happened. Complex problems must have simple explanations to gain political and shareholder support (which is often very difficult).

Here is a multi-prong approach to use to communicate shareholder information with both positive and negative information.

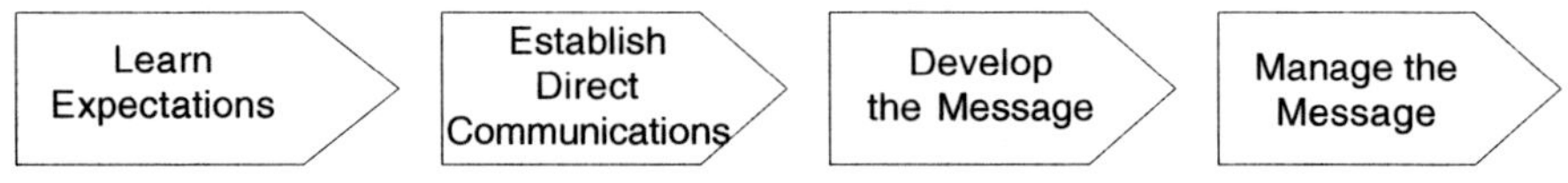

Dimension 1:
Identify shareholder and customer expectations upfront

- Learn the "Why" (Why are they interested in this situation?)
- Define the "When" (What triggered their interest?)
- Identify the "Who" (Exactly who is interested?)
- Provide the "How" (How are they reacting or responding?)
- Read hidden agendas (Why are some people upset and not others?)

Copyright © 2004, Idea Group Inc. Copying or distributing in print or electronic forms without written permission of Idea Group Inc. is prohibited.

- Bridge the client-shareholder gap (Put yourself in both of their shoes.)

Ask questions to extract answers if information is not volunteered or easily available. Listen to who is speaking, and understand why others are listening. Determine who enjoys the largest benefits or advantages and who has the smallest gains. Confirm your assumptions with all parties, as details may not be obvious.

Dimension 2:
Establishing direct communications channels

Why is this important? To avoid filtering or miscommunication of your message by others who may not have all of the information you may have. Communicating directly creates a single project "voice" that reduces the amount of confusion created by multiple perspectives for both good and bad news.

How can this be established?

- Publish a monthly IT security newsletter
- Build an organization IT security Web site having daily updates
- Become the "voice" all the time, everywhere
- Respond to questions on good news fast, and bad news faster

Dimension 3:
Develop the "message"

Know your audience — know what gets them interested and invested. Create a message that has a "What's in it for them" perspective from both the good news and bad news perspectives. If shareholders or customers will benefit from security improvements, let them know. It they will be negatively impacted financially or legally let them know.

Copyright © 2004, Idea Group Inc. Copying or distributing in print or electronic forms without written permission of Idea Group Inc. is prohibited.

Good messages "reach through" to the core issues faced by shareholders (image, financial impact and future growth) and customers (information privacy exposure, total loss, or access constraints). Learn what they get asked about from their customers or investors so that you can use their terminology. Keep the message brief and focused, and exclude specific dates, dollars or short-term issues that you are unclear about.

With good news, tell everyone why everything is going well, and the benefits or advantages to be recognized. With bad news, identify who is affected and who is not, possible causes, and possible solutions.

Dimension 4:
Manage the "message"

Determining the frequency, methods to use and opportunities to present updates to your message are key management decisions. With good news, announcements can usually be established to accommodate everyone's schedule. With bad news, there is never a good time to update shareholders and customers. Whenever there is enough accurate information to explain what happened, why it happened and what corrective action plans are being started is probably the earliest a message can be presented. Having accurate information is better than providing speculation based on fast changing assumptions.

If updates will be needed, tell the audience when they will be provided and in what format (presentation, e-mail, voicemail, Web site posting, etc.)

External factors may have an impact on the IT security scope and resources, which should be mentioned to shareholders and customers during presentations. There are situations that are completely outside any plausible planning events or scenarios, such as the September 11, 2001 attacks on the New York World Trade Center and the Pentagon.

Copyright © 2004, Idea Group Inc. Copying or distributing in print or electronic forms without written permission of Idea Group Inc. is prohibited.

Chapter III

Protecting Customer Provided Information

Charles Rex IV
National Defense University, USA

Introduction

Protecting customer provided information is crucial to the success of the organization. In order to maintain existing customers and attract new ones, firms must have a strategy to safeguard the information that the customers provide. The burden of responsibility is on the shoulders of the firm. The firm that demonstrates value to the customer and provides the most cost effective means of doing so will win in the competitive market.

Obviously, protecting customer provided information is a difficult task in the evolving and rapidly changing technological environment. However, it is a challenge that all firms must resolve to compete successfully in the marketplace. Ultimately, the executives and managers of an organization have a fiduciary responsibility to their stockholders to increase the value of the firm. The value of the firm increases as the customer base increases; however, security failures undermine this effort.

Copyright © 2004, Idea Group Inc. Copying or distributing in print or electronic forms without written permission of Idea Group Inc. is prohibited.

Accepting that information technology security is a winless game, managers and executives struggle to provide justification for security expenses that will not reveal an immediate return on investment. Coupled with this struggle is the complexity involved in identifying the vulnerabilities that exist in a dynamic environment and the *potential* threats that may or may not reveal themselves. It is difficult to balance the risks while justifying the value gained by investment in information security mechanisms. Extremes on either side of the continuum breed failure.

Protecting customer provided data spans further than merely the *customer-to-business* relationship; it extends to the *business-to-business* relationship along the entire supply chain, from distribution outlets to tiered suppliers. Security failures also may result in legal ramifications that could cripple the ability of the firm to function. Managing the security responsibility requires that firms design information assurance strategies that are dynamic in nature to match the evolving technological arena. These strategies are linked with proactive protective measures that must be flexible enough to cope with the rapidly changing environment.

Defining Customer Provided Information

What is customer provided information? Customer provided information is *all* information that the organization gains by any interaction with an existing or potential customer, as well as information on a customer that has been provided by an outside source. A partial list of this information may include: name, social security information, telephone number, address, age, sex, marital status, race, ethnicity, education, credit information, salary, family information, and employment data.

Copyright © 2004, Idea Group Inc. Copying or distributing in print or electronic forms without written permission of Idea Group Inc. is prohibited.

Numerous organizations maintain this type of information; for instance, the Internal Revenue Service (IRS) stores a tremendous quantity of information on their customers (taxpayers). The IRS obtains this information from employers. Although the IRS may not have obtained this information directly from the customer, it has a responsibility to protect the information.

Vulnerabilities and Threats

In layman terms, *vulnerability* is a shortcoming in the hardware or software of a computer or network system or a portal of entry into a computer or network system. Vulnerabilities are actually required to facilitate communication between two or more computers. If you communicate with another computer, you are ultimately making some type of change on the other computer system. While this action is desirable, it can also be exploited.

If vulnerability is exploited, it is a *threat* to the computer system or network. A threat is also a person or malicious computer system that seeks to cause harm to another computer system or network.

While there will always be vulnerabilities in computer systems and networks, there may not always be a threat. It is important to note that what may not be a vulnerability or threat at this time may not hold true in the future. Later in time, a once nonexistent vulnerability may suddenly emerge as a threat, especially as new technologies such as hardware and software upgrades are added to networked systems.

Copyright © 2004, Idea Group Inc. Copying or distributing in print or electronic forms without written permission of Idea Group Inc. is prohibited.

Shareholder Wealth

The electronic commerce marketplace thrives on interconnected relationships. Firms that fail to embrace electronic commerce have been replaced or are treading water to stay afloat. Global competition has changed the economy of all markets. Firms no longer have the option to go back to their old ways of doing business. You cannot put the genie back into the bottle, and Pandora's box has already been opened.

There is a cyclical relationship between customers and investors. As a firm gains customers, the value of the firm increases. As the value of the firm increases, the firm becomes more appealing in profitability to investors. The executives and managers of a firm therefore have a fiduciary responsibility to make decisions that increase the value of a firm.

Security failures cause havoc on this relationship. Unfortunately, many firms only embrace security efforts after the damage has already been done. These problems usually show their face as denial-of-service attacks, viruses, and e-mail problems. This list can go on and on; however, sometimes the attacks go largely unnoticed, at least initially. Unfortunately, unnoticed attacks are sometimes the most damaging in scope as in the following example:

In 2001, 32-year-old Abraham Abdullah duped more than 200 of Forbes "400 Richest People in America" by stealing their identities. Mr. Abdullah collected information on individuals by using a publicly accessible computer at a Brooklyn, New York library to hack into databases that contained personal information from some of the world's most prestigious credit companies. He used this information to fraudulently open credit accounts, ultimately stealing more than $80 million dollars. It took authorities more than six months to apprehend Abdullah. At the time of his apprehension, the authorities found more

Copyright © 2004, Idea Group Inc. Copying or distributing in print or electronic forms without written permission of Idea Group Inc. is prohibited.

than 800 fraudulent credit cards and 20,000 blank credit cards among his belongings.

An attack of this magnitude can be devastating to a firm. The security failures of firms can have many grave implications. Usually at the top of the list would be an obvious loss of customers. Today's customers are rapidly being apprised of the implications of the lackadaisical security measures. If one of your customers becomes a target of such an attack due to the inadequate security measures taken by your firm, they will likely discontinue the relationship. The value of the firm may decrease and ultimately fail.

It would seem that to prevent such a scenario from happening, executives and managers would simply "protect" the security posture. Unfortunately, it is not quite that simple; it is not just a matter of having security or not having security. First, it is nearly impossible to eliminate all vulnerabilities. It is an impossible proposition because technology is constantly evolving. Networked systems are designed to communicate with other systems. As long as systems communicate with one another, they will have vulnerabilities because the communication process itself requires that each system have the ability to exchange information with others. In addition, investment in technology security is extremely costly. These costs usually do not render an immediate tangible return on investment; quite the contrary, they usually render an immediate negative on the bottom line, making investment unappealing.

Although the financial cost to protect information technology systems and the information that they contain is a costly proposition, they are necessary. Choosing *not to protect* may be even more costly in the end because customers will stop doing business with the firm. Understanding that *doing nothing* is not an option allows the firm to build a strategy to push forward to protect the assets. From the forefront, it is necessary to understand that the investment in security technology will require significant fiscal resources, and the return on

Copyright © 2004, Idea Group Inc. Copying or distributing in print or electronic forms without written permission of Idea Group Inc. is prohibited.

investment will be largely intangible. Taking a stepped, 360-degree approach to information assurance will reveal surprising results, however.

In the *business-to-business* relationship arena, firms are recognizing that technological security is integral to success. Businesses are beginning to focus on protecting their assets, and in doing so, recognize that vulnerabilities exist whenever they conduct transactions with other businesses. The technological innovations that have rapidly found their place in the market, such as electronic data interchange (EDI), enterprise resource planning (ERP) systems, and customer relationship management (CRM) systems, have forced businesses to incorporate their business partners within their security strategies. Businesses must have some form of reassurance that their partners in the market also have security mechanisms in place so that potential threats can be staved off, thus mitigating the vulnerabilities that exist between the technologically interconnected firms.

The interconnected relationship between firms goes largely unnoticed until something goes wrong. Suppliers are typically interconnected through EDI with the manufacturing or service providing firms. This electronic connection has enabled firms to cut overhead costs associated with inventory control, supply specification, shipping, and so forth. The EDI connection usually spans several tiers throughout the supply chain. Within the manufacturing or service providing firm, ERP systems have enabled them to optimize their operations, ensuring that resources are available to conduct operations seamlessly. EDI and ERP systems are also interconnected with the distribution outlets for the goods or services that the firm renders. The actual customer and distribution outlets are sometimes interconnected with one another through CRM technologies. As illustrated, throughout the entire supply chain, from customer to supplier, all can be interconnected through technological innovation. This interconnected relationship presents

Copyright © 2004, Idea Group Inc. Copying or distributing in print or electronic forms without written permission of Idea Group Inc. is prohibited.

numerous vulnerabilities. While the vulnerabilities exist, not all will be exploited by threats. Firms must be able to determine which vulnerabilities are critical to their continued operations. Those critical vulnerabilities should be protected first, while other less critical vulnerabilities can be protected later.

Maintaining and Increasing the Customer Base

Customers will do business with firms that are reputable, provide the products or services they demand at a reasonable cost, and are accommodating and user friendly. In the context of the global marketplace, customers can transact business with virtually any firm in the world. In the past, consumers did not have the same opportunities. Businesses were insulated from global competition by geography, currencies, and languages. The same no longer holds true in today's market.

In order to be reputable, a firm must provide quality products or services and they must have a proven performance record. Failures in these areas spread like wildfire in the Internet Age. At the touch of a button, company records can be obtained. The convenience of the global market also has fostered stiffer competition among firms. Customers can now shop for products from a multitude of firms for the most competitive price. The ease of the buying experience also influences the mindset of a customer. In combination, these criteria can make or break a sale. If a firm fails in any aspect, the likelihood of retaining or attracting business from the customer becomes questionable.

Customers must be reassured that their information is important to the business and will be safeguarded as such. For instance, for an online transaction, it is necessary that the firm have security mechanisms to protect the customer's credit card transaction during transmission over

Copyright © 2004, Idea Group Inc. Copying or distributing in print or electronic forms without written permission of Idea Group Inc. is prohibited.

the Internet. Security measures such as secure servers and private Internet sessions can facilitate this objective. Once the information has been obtained from the customer, the information must be protected. Customer confidence is the objective.

Professional Responsibility

Security failures do occur. Firms that have not fallen into the clutches of an attack are rare. Even individual computer users are familiar with some to the damaging repercussions of insufficient security measures. Computer viruses wreak havoc on computer systems, executing worms and Trojan Horses into systems, damaging computer code, and costing hours of frustration. This vulnerability is costly to a single computer, but the cost becomes exponential in massive networked infrastructures. Millions of dollars a day can be lost due to these attacks in some institutions.

Organizations in both the public and private sector also face another challenge when their system vulnerabilities are exploited. That challenge is whether to report the attack to the authorities and whether to release information regarding the attack to the general public.

Reporting security incidents to the authorities is sensitive in nature. While the firm may need all the assistance they can possibly obtain, the authorities have a legal obligation to record and report the incident for investigation and auditing purposes. The Federal Bureau of Investigation (FBI) is usually the leading investigating body for cyber crime incidents in the private sector. The private sector also employs private cyber forensic investigation teams to assist in eliminating and securing the infrastructure. The public sector also utilizes the FBI, but governmental organizations that have a stake in national security must alert the National Security Agency (NSA).

Copyright © 2004, Idea Group Inc. Copying or distributing in print or electronic forms without written permission of Idea Group Inc. is prohibited.

Many Computer Emergency Response Teams (CERTs) have been established worldwide to assist organizations in recovering from computer attacks. Both the public and private sectors employ the CERTs. They are most valuable during the initial attacks on automated systems. Various cyber forensic techniques are initiated by the CERTs to identify the attacker and provide guidance on eliminating the immediate threat.

Reporting intrusions and attacks to the public is also sensitive. Publicizing security failures can have detrimental affects. While there is some argument that the organization has a professional responsibility to report failures to protect the customer's interest, there are also legitimate arguments that contradict such reporting maneuvers. Reporting security vulnerability, in itself, may cause an escalation in similar attacks on the very same vulnerability.

The firm must also take into account that reporting a security breach may result in a loss of customer and investor confidence. If customer and investor confidence evaporate quickly, not only would the firm be scrabbling to patch the holes in their security enclave, but would also be struggling to reassure customers and investors that counteractive measures are being undertaken to prevent continued and future attacks. Timid knee-jerk reactions by customers and investors will only compound and prolong the difficulties.

Firms that are interconnected with supply chain partners also have a responsibility to notify their partners of the security breach to limit potentially damaging security vulnerabilities from spreading to their partners.

The Harvard Business School case study scenario: *The iPremier Company (A): Denial of Service Attack* illustrates the chaos that ensues during a security failure within a firm. Although this scenario is not an actual event, the actions taken in this case are strikingly similar to the actions taken by firms during an initial cyber attack. It would be

Copyright © 2004, Idea Group Inc. Copying or distributing in print or electronic forms without written permission of Idea Group Inc. is prohibited.

advisable to obtain a copy of the case scenario as a training document for all levels within an organization (Austin, 2001).

Security is a Winless Game

When nothing happens, it is a good thing from the security perspective. However, justifying *nothing* is a difficult proposition to sell to upper management, executives, members of the board, and shareholders. Traditionally, we have been taught that success usually means that *something has happened.* Retooling our measurement toolkit to incorporate *nothing* as being a good thing is difficult at best. The Department of Homeland Security (DHS) faces a similar measurement obstacle. If nothing happens, DHS is successful. This mindset is difficult to visualize because success in the traditional sense is usually defined as improvement through quantifiable financial measures.

Quantifiable measures can be obtained in a robust security posture, however. Although the quantifiable measures are not in financial terms, the number of potential attacks that have been successfully defended can explain them. A good security mechanism is capable of collecting information on these potential attacks. Security status reports should focus on both the successes of these defenses and the failures.

Maintaining a robust security posture is also never-ending. The technological environment is dynamic, and thus, the security mechanism must change with emerging technologies. Executives and board members alike will fret over the endless investment in securing the infrastructure. This is security, however, and that is just the name of the game.

Technological change has transformed the face of the marketplace. It has enabled firms to compete in markets that never before existed, in ways that were never even imagined a decade ago. Employees can now work by telecommuting, never needing an office at a

Copyright © 2004, Idea Group Inc. Copying or distributing in print or electronic forms without written permission of Idea Group Inc. is prohibited.

downtown location. They can also work from virtually anywhere in the world from a portable computer the size of a laptop or even a personal digital assistant (PDA) that can fit in the palm of your hand. With this flexibility also come vulnerability and an increase in threats.

The security infrastructure is only as good as its trusted agents. In other words, imagine that you have a laptop that has an encryption enabled virtual private network (VPN) client that allows you to establish a secure tunnel connection to your businesses network, and security certificates or tokens unique to the specific computer. While this security mechanism is robust by most standards, imagine utilizing the laptop while in a different country, using telecommunication lines that may be subject to monitoring by interested parties. Transactions over those lines are subject to monitoring and possibly even exploitation. The potential for a security breach is self-explanatory.

Imagine once again the same laptop with the same security mechanisms being pilfered by a thief. If the thief has malicious intent and is computer savvy, it is also possible that the security mechanism could be breached. The trusted agent, the laptop computer in this case, represents a serious threat to the seemingly robust security infrastructure.

Expanding this subject even further, imagine a customer conducting business with your firm. In this case, the customer is not overly computer savvy, but knows enough to perform a business transaction over the Internet. However, the customer does not have a firewall enabled on their computer. The customer utilizes a broadband connection, so they are continuously connected to the Internet and have become accustomed to leaving their computer on except during thunderstorms. Little do they know that a hacker has been *sniffing* packets on their computer and has loaded a program onto their operating system allowing the hacker to hijack a session at their whim. Since the customer has established a session with your network, a clear path to your sensitive data is open for the taking. The hacker hijacks the

Copyright © 2004, Idea Group Inc. Copying or distributing in print or electronic forms without written permission of Idea Group Inc. is prohibited.

customer's session and begins to exploit your computer systems. Depending on the security mechanisms in place at your firm, you may or may not even notice the attack and may or may not be able to defend against it.

The low cost of installing wireless local area networks (WLANs) makes it an attractive alternative to firms. Considering that many firms utilize leased office spaces and are accustomed to moving to new spaces every couple of years, WLAN infrastructures are a convenient, cost effective, and flexible alternative to the costly, installation intrusive, and permanent Ethernet wired local area network (LAN) infrastructure. Wireless networks, however, are extremely vulnerable. No longer is the firm simply able to protect unauthorized use of the network by utilizing physical security mechanisms like security guards and locked doors. Now, the firm must secure the radio waves that have replaced the wired network infrastructurc. It is similar to "installing an Ethernet jack in the parking lot" (Reid & Seide, 2003). WLAN infrastructure must be protected with the same resolve as that taken with any network.

Securing information on computer networks has many pitfalls. Sometimes organizations suffer from knee-jerk reactions after they have been exploited by an attack. Firms may fall into the trap of over-expenditure in computer security. Inexperienced firms may invest heavily in security measures that, for the immediate threat are top-of-the-line, but find that six months down the road the security mechanism is incapable of defending against new attacks. They have so crippled their resource budgets that it is impossible to invest in newer security technologies to improve defenses. They begin to feel as though they have purchased a *boat;* nothing more than a hole in the water into which you pour money. Even if fiscal resources were not a constraint, without a long-term security strategy, all the money in the world may not render the desired results.

Copyright © 2004, Idea Group Inc. Copying or distributing in print or electronic forms without written permission of Idea Group Inc. is prohibited.

Yet another pitfall that firms often fall into is that of a false sense of security. This pitfall is known as the "September 11th Syndrome". In this pitfall, firms assume that since they have never suffered from an attack in the past that they are protected from attacks in the future. They may also believe that their computer systems do not have sensitive customer and operational data residing on them, yet in reality, they have many data records that are now entrenched in their day-to-day operational business processes but do not realize it. Many Mom and Pop's are just as vulnerable as *Fortune 500* companies are.

Keep in mind: some of the most damaging attacks are those that go unnoticed. Malicious hackers may be exploiting networked systems collecting sensitive customer data on a continuous basis. The repercussions of such an attack can be exponential and irreversible. Depending on the scope and nature of the attack, a firm could potentially be brought to its knees in a single day.

Vulnerabilities and threats are constantly growing and evolving. Keeping up with emerging technologies is challenging enough, but also keeping up with threats that are not even known is even more difficult. Hackers come in many forms, from the mischievous 12-year-old, known as a *kiddy,* to the educated and refined professional hacker or terrorist that has malicious intent; the range of sophistication is near infinite. Yet, there is also a common distinction amongst threats: whether they are internal or external threats.

The common assumption of most is that external threats are the most pervasive. However, that assumption is severely flawed. The most common threats are from internal sources. Everyone within your organization, including the top executives, network administrators, customer service personnel, administrative staff, physical plant maintenance crews, and cleaning personnel, represents internal threats. Many of these personnel have unimpeded access to customer information sources. While access control mechanisms can eliminate many of the

Copyright © 2004, Idea Group Inc. Copying or distributing in print or electronic forms without written permission of Idea Group Inc. is prohibited.

internal threats, ultimately, some personnel will have complete access to data stored on the firm's computer systems. While this may be undesirable, it may be unavoidable. For example, the network administrators at many firms have complete access to all data repositories. They often need this access by task necessity to ensure that the day-to-day operations of the firm are possible. How trustworthy is your firm's network administrator?

The thought of an internal threat is detestable and distasteful in any light. The implication of such a threat affects the organizational culture, climate, and value system to its very foundation. Employees will not look favorably upon the constant monitoring of their day-to-day activities. Employees are often left feeling as if they owe the firm no allegiance if the firm itself does not even trust them enough to do their work in privacy and confidence. Yet, the firm is caught between a rock and a hard place because failurc to monitor the activities of their employees is a huge liability.

External sources pose a smaller yet no less detestable threat. External threats face significant challenges in successfully gaining access to computer systems because they do not have the benefit of being insiders. Any security mechanism that is enabled on a computer system requires time to overcome. Sometimes hackers will simply avoid systems that require significant contributions of their time to penetrate. It is much easier to wreak havoc on systems with lackadaisical security. In reality, the path of least resistance renders the most economy to the malicious hacker.

Just as there are distinctions between internal and external threats, there are also distinctions between the objectives of the threats. Some hackers only intend to disrupt the ability of the firm to conduct business. An example of such an attack would be a distributed denial-of-service attack, which clogs the computer's ability to process instructions, thus limiting its ability to perform critical operations and potentially bringing

Copyright © 2004, Idea Group Inc. Copying or distributing in print or electronic forms without written permission of Idea Group Inc. is prohibited.

the network to a standstill. Others simply seek to crack into the network to browse the resources to gain recognition from other hackers through bragging rights. Still other hackers maliciously attack computer systems to access sensitive company or customer data such as financial records and credit card information or seek to cause serious damage. Obviously, the malicious attacker poses the most significant threat to the business.

Fine Line between Clever and Stupid

The movie *This is Spinal Tap* holds one of the best lines of all time: "there's a fine line between clever and stupid" (Reiner, 1984). This line holds true in the business world as well, especially in the context of information security and assurance. Striking the right balance is often more of an art form than one of pure science. It is necessary that every firm determine what exactly is *stupid* and what is *clever.*

What is stupid? One way to begin the process of defining what is stupid is by working backwards, almost as a reverse engineering exercise of sorts. A computer system that is 100% secure means that it is 100% inaccessible by a network and thus useless. As can be deduced, this predicament does not possess the desired security qualities. If customers and partners in the supply chain find that it is impossible to connect with the firm, then they will abandon their attempts and seek to do business with others.

To define what is *clever,* the firm must work to determine what level of security provides the firm the best security posture with an acceptable level of risk. Performing a detailed risk assessment involves looking at the technical specifications of the network infrastructure and marrying that information with the requirements of the actual business operations. This information includes requirements of the unique busi-

Copyright © 2004, Idea Group Inc. Copying or distributing in print or electronic forms without written permission of Idea Group Inc. is prohibited.

ness functions, operational requirements, core competencies, mission, and an understanding of customer demands. Identification of the vulnerabilities of the infrastructure can be identified and paired with the predominate threats, and then evaluated against the operational requirements.

These data are collected and analyzed through a risk assessment process. It is imperative that during the risk assessment processes, most, if not all, functional area experts are represented so that unique and critical operational requirements are identified and maintained for the continued operations of the firm. The identified vulnerabilities and threats are then evaluated to determine which represent the highest priority. This priority is typically tied to their mission criticality.

Vulnerabilities and threats that, if exploited, could bring business operations to a halt should be given the highest priority. Those vulnerabilities and threats that cause only minimal and insignificant impact, or are not likely to be exploited should be given the lowest priority. After the vulnerabilities and threats have been assigned a priority, mitigating strategies can be designed to minimize or eliminate the vulnerabilities and threats with consideration of the operational and financial impacts of implementing such security mechanisms.

Seal of Approval

It is evident that in today's interconnected electronic and global economy that information assurance and security poses a significant issue to all organizations. There have been numerous discussions and forums, in both the public and private sectors, specifically on the challenges that organizations face today concerning the subject. Given that businesses face significant vulnerabilities due largely to their

Copyright © 2004, Idea Group Inc. Copying or distributing in print or electronic forms without written permission of Idea Group Inc. is prohibited.

interconnectedness with one another, transacting business with a firm that does not employ robust security mechanisms is a huge liability.

One suggestion that has surfaced is the establishment of a security rating for firms. The security rating would be set up similar to the "well-known Underwriters Laboratories ... (t)he goal would be to certify that a business has governance policies and technical infrastructure procedures in place to make that business a more secure company" (Beach, 2003). Such a security rating would serve as a reassurance not only to other firms that there is some assurance that their supply chain partners are secure but also may reassure customers that their information is protected.

Such a certifying body would have the role of assessing the infrastructures of firms based on evolving security and assurance standards. It could also serve as a clearinghouse for best practices in information security and assurance, assisting firms in implementing security strategies in stepped progressions.

Obtaining certification would be a voluntary action initiated by the firm requesting the certification rating.

The certifying body would not have any enforcement role, but it could operate as a body that could confer a security rating status based on the mechanisms in place. A periodic security audit term must be established to ensure that the certification has teeth. A periodic recertification every two years would be advisable after the initial term.

Legal Ramifications

Maintaining customer provided information carries with it a significant legal responsibility. As such, customer records are a significant liability. However, they are also a significant asset. One reason to maintain customer information is because it is needed to perform a

Copyright © 2004, Idea Group Inc. Copying or distributing in print or electronic forms without written permission of Idea Group Inc. is prohibited.

transaction with the customer in the first place, and it can assist the firm in obtaining repeat business from the customer in the future.

Customers should expect a degree of confidentiality and privacy when conducting business with both the public and private sectors. They should be assured that their sensitive information would not be released to other parties. Some of this assurance is codified in the Privacy Act of 1974.

The law extends further in reference to securing customer provided information, which will be covered in detail later in this book. Some of the codified laws that pertain specifically to the protection of customer provided data include the Government Performance and Results Act of 1993, Paperwork Reduction Act of 1995, Clinger-Cohen Act of 1996, Digital Millennium Copyright Act of 1998, U.S. Government Information Security Reform Act of 2000, Digital Signatures Act of 2000, USA Patriot Act of 2001, E-Government Act of 2002, and the Sarbanes-Oxley Act of 2002.

Security failures could — and increasingly do — lead to customer litigation. Inadequately protecting customer provided data from unauthorized disclosure due to security failures may result in liability findings by the courts. To prevent such findings, it is imperative that firms initiate a plan of action for implementing an information assurance strategy.

Designing an Information Assurance Strategy

Now that you are aware of the vulnerabilities and threats and the implications of acting or failing to act, you need to design a strategy that recognizes the firm's operational requirements and pairs those requirements with the necessity to protect the assets inherent to the firm and its customers while mitigating exposure to entities that wish to cause harm.

Copyright © 2004, Idea Group Inc. Copying or distributing in print or electronic forms without written permission of Idea Group Inc. is prohibited.

An information assurance strategy is comprised of several independent yet interrelated action plans: the firm's strategic plan, contingency operations plan, the disaster recovery plan, and the infrastructure security plan.

First, the firm's strategic plan is integral. This plan outlines the "roadmap" that guides the firm into the future. This plan should contain information that identifies future initiatives and requirements, the core competencies, the vision of how the firm will satisfy the demands of its customers, financial expectations, the roles that departmental structures play, and the expectations of the stakeholders and how the firm will integrate those expectations with their performance goals.

Second, the contingency operations plan (COOP) outlines in detail how the firm will operate in the event of a change in the operational posture of the firm. It focuses on the details of how the firm will operate in the event of a natural or man-made disaster, or terrorist event. The plan specifies alternate work locations and accompanying infrastructure design, remote telecommuting plans, required hardware and software inventories, procurement strategies, key emergency personnel contact rosters, and data accessibility requirements.

Third, the disaster recovery plan identifies the critical technological resources and approach for restoring access to the information stored on such devices. It outlines the strategy to procure resources and critical milestones that must be accomplished to recover from the disaster. The critical technological resources are prioritized and target recovery timelines are established. These critical resources represent the minimum resources that are necessary to continue the operations of the firm.

Care should be taken when designing the disaster recovery plan. Organizations tend to priorities all resources as being critical when, in fact, they are not critical in the overall perspective. It is important only to identify those resources that must be restored to continue operations.

Copyright © 2004, Idea Group Inc. Copying or distributing in print or electronic forms without written permission of Idea Group Inc. is prohibited.

Interdependencies of automated systems should also be identified in this plan and matched to the appropriate criticality priority.

Fourth, the infrastructure security plan identifies the known vulnerabilities and threats to the existing network infrastructure. This plan, as with the preceding plans, should be a living document. As new hardware and software are implemented within the network, the plan should be adjusted to embrace any new vulnerabilities and threats. It details the mitigating strategies and security mechanisms that are in place within the firm. It also includes a 100% inventory of all technological assets, as well as all telecommunication connections.

The information assurance plan incorporates all of the above resources at a minimum. Depending on the unique requirements of the specific firm, additional plans should be incorporated into the information assurance plan. Overall, the information assurance plan outlines a comprehensive strategy for securing the firm in any setting to assure unimpeded continued operations. Key timeframes should be identified, such as the target hour for restoring partial operations and timeline for the restoration of all operational capabilities.

This information assurance plan should have the widest dissemination throughout the firm. Modification to the plan should be distributed and periodic review of the plan should occur at regular intervals. Typically, a moderate review should be performed annually, and a clean-slate review should be performed every three years.

The information assurance strategy should include a security audit. This audit should examine the above documented plans and ensure their accuracy and current applicability in the existing infrastructure. The audit may also include penetration testing performed by a disinterested examination body. The scope of penetration testing is variable depending on the needs of the firm. Results of the penetration testing should be held in strict confidence and should be performed unannounced to employees with the exception of the senior executives, including the

Copyright © 2004, Idea Group Inc. Copying or distributing in print or electronic forms without written permission of Idea Group Inc. is prohibited.

information security officer. Preempted disclosure of the penetration test will reveal skewed results.

Feedback based on the security audit and penetration testing should be examined, and resolution strategies should be initiated to mitigate security vulnerabilities if representative of critical failures.

Protective Security Measures

Implementing protective security measures begins with the employees. As discussed earlier, the largest threat to information security originates from internal sources. Implementing hardware and software security measures will have little effective impact in securing the infrastructure if the internal threats are present.

Education Programs

It is necessary to educate the employees of the organization. An approach to educating the employees is through a stepped education model. This model is comprised of several *steps* of education and training.

The first step is usually designed as a *broad stroke* to capture and articulate the purposes and strategy behind securing information. It should include basic techniques that all users should abide by and the repercussions for failures in compliance. At the conclusion of this training, it is advisable to have employees sign user agreements that specify acceptable and unacceptable computer use and prohibited activities.

The second step is usually tailored toward the functional perspective. This training should cover the functional and departmental specific security actions that employees must take to minimize security threats.

Copyright © 2004, Idea Group Inc. Copying or distributing in print or electronic forms without written permission of Idea Group Inc. is prohibited.

Other training should be designed that educates information security officers within each department and network operations personnel. The network operation personnel should be trained continuously on information security strategies that are up-to-date on the current threats and vulnerabilities.

Security Officer Appointments

A chief information security officer (CISO) should be appointed who is responsible for designing and monitoring the information assurance strategy of the firm. It is recommended that this officer not be the designated chief information officer or information management officer to avoid conflicts of interest. The CISO should report to the chief executive or director of the organization.

The Security Enclave

A security enclave is comprised of the infrastructure components within a firm that is protected by security mechanisms. The security mechanisms protect the enclave from both electronic intrusions, as well as from physical intrusions by unauthorized entities.

Security guards and doorway control mechanisms such as locks can protect physical intrusions, and by placing computer operation centers that store data records in areas that are not easily accessed by windows or doorways in plain view.

Employing a combination of hardware and software mechanisms can protect electronic intrusions. These security mechanisms must be planned in detail to work effectively. Since implementing all the components of a security mechanism is costly and complex, it is advisable to implement the measures in a stepped progression. Measures that address the broadest spectrum of vulnerabilities are usually the most

Copyright © 2004, Idea Group Inc. Copying or distributing in print or electronic forms without written permission of Idea Group Inc. is prohibited.

effective means of securing the infrastructure. Examples of such a broad stroke include antivirus programs and firewalls. These measures are typically the foundational steps in building the enclave. Once they have been effectively implemented, further steps can be taken to fortify the enclave, such as installing access control mechanisms, intrusion detection systems, and so forth.

The brief descriptions below explain the major components of a security enclave.

Antivirus Protection Software

Antivirus protection software represents the bare minimum of every security enclave. Antivirus software is usually installed on every client computer. The antivirus software signature files must be maintained up-to-date on a regular basis to work effectively.

Software Management Servers

Software management servers (SMS) serve the purpose of pushing operating system software updates to client computers located on the network. The operating system software must be maintained up-to-date to limit the vulnerabilities that are discovered on a continuous basis by the manufacturers. When update patches are available from the manufacturer, the SMS can push these updates to each machine, ensuring that the latest version of the operating system is utilized.

Firewalls

Firewalls are security mechanisms that grant or prevent access to internal resources requested from outside the security enclave such as the Internet. Firewalls are similar to a gangplank of a ship. Users that

Copyright © 2004, Idea Group Inc. Copying or distributing in print or electronic forms without written permission of Idea Group Inc. is prohibited.

hold the requisite authorization to access resources inside the enclave are granted access. Users that do not have the requisite authorization are denied access to the resources inside the enclave. Firewalls are in two forms and are often used in conjunction with one another. One form of firewall is an actual piece of computer hardware. The other form is software based. Firewalls can also be configured on individual client machines. This type of firewall is ideal for users that work remotely outside the firm's security enclave.

Access Control Mechanisms

Access control mechanisms serve the purpose of requiring users to present credentials before being granted access to information resources inside the security enclave. The access control mechanism is usually comprised of a server loaded with an access control application. The access control mechanism is often transparent to users. Typically, users are issued credentials based on user role groups. Access control can also be configured to require authentication during each session, usually in the form of a username and password combination. Successful username and password combinations are granted access to the requested resources. Access control mechanisms are effective in deterring data theft from unauthorized internal and external threats.

Intrusion Detection Systems

Intrusion Detection Systems (IDS) are extremely effective when regularly monitored and configured properly. The inter-workings of intrusion detection systems are highly guarded and should be held in strict confidence. Most IDS systems record all transactions within the security enclave and requests from outside the enclave. Trend analysis

Copyright © 2004, Idea Group Inc. Copying or distributing in print or electronic forms without written permission of Idea Group Inc. is prohibited.

is performed on the transaction logs to identify inconsistencies and/or irregular activities and transactions. Additional scrutiny is placed on network transactions from outside the security enclave. Intrusion detection systems are effective in deterring data theft from unauthorized internal and external threats.

Encryption Mechanisms

Encryption mechanisms serve to protect data during transmission. Encryption applications must be installed and configured on both the sending and receiving computer. During a data transmission, the sending computer encrypts the data before transmitting. Upon receipt of the encrypted data, the receiving computer decrypts the data. Encryption mechanisms are based on numerous proprietary algorithms. The more complex the algorithm, the more secure the data transmission; however, the performance of the computer will degrade with an increase in algorithmic complexity. Encryption mechanisms are effective against *packet sniffing* outside the security enclave.

Network Disconnect Devices

Network disconnect devices are mechanisms that immediately disconnect telecommunications between the security enclave and the external environment. In the event of an intrusion or denial-of-service attack, telecommunications can be disconnected immediately without causing serious damage to the network systems inside the enclave. Network disconnect devices serve the same effect as physically unplugging telecommunications or powering down computer equipment without causing serious damage and data loss. Network disconnect devices are usually comprised of both hardware and software in a single unit. Control of the disconnect command is usually activated

Copyright © 2004, Idea Group Inc. Copying or distributing in print or electronic forms without written permission of Idea Group Inc. is prohibited.

manually or by threshold signals from intrusion detection systems. While the security enclave is disconnected, the organization cannot communicate outside the enclave but it can enable the security professionals to diagnose and possibly resolve the vulnerability to defend against the threat before reconnecting telecommunications.

Conclusions

Protecting customer provided information is a complex and challenging feat. However, organizations must provide the assurance of confidentiality to their customers if they are to survive in the global electronic marketplace. Not only do organizations have a legal requirement to safeguard this information, but they also have a professional responsibility to their business partners in the supply chain.

Information security is a winless game by traditional measures, but effective implementation can reveal long-term rewards and success.

Although information security is a constantly evolving and dynamic game, by implementing detailed and comprehensive information assurance strategies, organizations can make sound decisions to preserve their place in the market while defending against threats.

Copyright © 2004, Idea Group Inc. Copying or distributing in print or electronic forms without written permission of Idea Group Inc. is prohibited.

Chapter IV

Global IT Risk Management Strategies

Chrisan Herrod
National Defense University, USA

Introduction

This chapter describes why it is important for organizations to develop and implement an IT risk management function and use best practice risk assessment methodologies that provide a standard to measure and assess risk within organizations. Information technology risk management is a significant new function that can help companies achieve world class IT service. IT risk management includes regulatory compliance, information security, disaster recovery, and project risks. IT risk management should be part of a company's risk management strategy on an equal footing with financial risk management and reputational risk management. As the complexity of IT infrastructures increases and as businesses continue to rely upon the Internet as the communication backbone for e-business, the associated risks increase. For these reasons, deciding upon and implementing a risk management process and a standard methodology will greatly reduce the risks associated with the introduction of new technologies that support the mission of the business.

Copyright © 2004, Idea Group Inc. Copying or distributing in print or electronic forms without written permission of Idea Group Inc. is prohibited.

The inherent complexities of developing, deploying and managing IT services on a global scale are obvious. Add to these the legislative and regulatory framework that govern business practices in many industries, and companies are faced with a situation where only constant vigilance can ensure they are operating safely and legally. Peril cannot be eliminated from the business life cycle, and failures can result in loss, injuries, and lawsuits. At the same time, IT is essential to the success of any business. Many opportunities arise from exploiting information technologies in ways that advance business and serve customers.

The goal of an IT risk management organization should be to ensure potential risks are identified and assessed and, where the business considers it necessary, to implement controls that mitigate the potential impact of the risk. This is achieved by:

- Creating **Policy**
- Making **Process** improvements
- Defining **Procedures or Standards**
- Instituting controls through **Management Practices**
- Following **Guidelines**
- Building **Contracts**
- Using groups in the **Organization**
- **Outsourcing** where necessary
- **Insuring** against the consequences

Risk Management Defined

Risk is an uncertain event or condition that, if it occurs, may have a negative effect on activities being performed in the business. Risk management is the systematic process of identifying risk, assessing the likelihood of its occurring and the impact it may have, and taking the

Copyright © 2004, Idea Group Inc. Copying or distributing in print or electronic forms without written permission of Idea Group Inc. is prohibited.

action necessary to ensure that the reward from the activities performed will be realized.

Risk management is the balancing of risk and reward to ensure that rewards are maximized and risks are minimized to a degree acceptable to the business.

Key to Risk Management Success

The key for risk management is to identify and manage risks so the reward being sought exceeds the impact of the risks encountered. This task is impossible unless the risks are identified. Those that are not identified and handled appropriately may create the most damage.

Understanding the Dynamics of Risk

Whenever a business introduces change, a dynamic that affects risk is also introduced. Change has the potential for increasing or decreasing risk. Most change has an associated reward, which is why a business is willing to confront risks that might be incurred.

Risk management starts with the monitoring of projects and programs and other external and internal factors that may create risk. A business change will often generate multiple potential risks. Each risk may affect multiple business units or functional areas.

Responses to Risk

The response to the introduction of risk can result in one of the following decisions.

- *Mitigate a Risk.* Where steps are taken to reduce the probability of a risk maturing (occurring), or reducing the impact or loss should that risk mature.

Copyright © 2004, Idea Group Inc. Copying or distributing in print or electronic forms without written permission of Idea Group Inc. is prohibited.

- *Avoid a Risk.* Where the decision is made to avoid taking the risk. Typically, this means the reward/benefit to the company cannot be acquired.
- *Transfer a Risk.* Where the anticipated loss of the maturing risk is transferred to another party. Typically, this would be a third party (e.g., insurance against lawsuit).
- *Accept a Risk.* Where no steps are taken to either mitigate, avoid or transfer the risk. Basically, in accepting a risk, the company has chosen to accept the consequences should the risk mature.

Risk Management Framework

The decision to respond to risk should be based on the use of a standard risk management methodology or framework. Decisions about the way risk is managed should not be made in isolation and definitely not be made without some due diligence. A risk management framework provides a process which if followed results in a logical basis for making decisions. Facts and data are collected and presented in a rational manner.

There are many risk management methodologies in use both in the public and private sector. One is not better than the other; frameworks such as the one proposed in this chapter should be adapted to fit the environment and/or the culture of the business. Typically key principals guide a risk management framework:

- Risk and its impact should be viewed holistically — that is, from the perspective of the entire business. Assessing the impact of risk from a more narrow perspective poses risks in its own right since business needs may outweigh a negative IT impact.
- Risks are only significant if they have a business impact or quantifiable loss.

Copyright © 2004, Idea Group Inc. Copying or distributing in print or electronic forms without written permission of Idea Group Inc. is prohibited.

- The framework must provide a basis for the evaluation of all kinds of risk, from minor security incidents to potentially catastrophic events.
- It may sometimes be necessary to handle incidents before studying the driver that causes them to occur — treating risks holistically does not mean we let the business collapse before fixing the problem!

Scalability of Risk Management Processes

The approach to risk management needs to be scalable to address different sizes and sources of risk. Typically, this may involve using the risk management framework in different ways, possibly beginning from different starting points.

Scalability should address each of the following sources of risk:

- *Major Business Risks.* Mergers, acquisitions, introduction of new e-business sites and opportunities, legislation, legal issues.
- *Key IT Risks.* Introduction of new technologies supporting business processes, whether internal or external.
- *Project Risks.*
  - Risks to business continuity introduced by a project
  - Risks to the benefits realization of a project (risks to achieving benefits of project)
  - Risk to successful project delivery.
- *Individual Risks & Incidents.* Inherent in work and practices involving use and practice of IT.

Copyright © 2004, Idea Group Inc. Copying or distributing in print or electronic forms without written permission of Idea Group Inc. is prohibited.

Risk Management is Everyone's Responsibility

As risk is inherent in everything a business does, risk management must be a part of everyone's job if the business goals are to be fully realized. Threats to the company's goals have to be minimized, at least to the point where the rewards sought as a business outweigh the likely impact of the threats.

In order to assess if risk is being managed properly, ask the following questions:

- Are you familiar with the business processes that support daily work? Do you know the reward associated with those following those processes?
- Do you understand which IT controls (policies, processes, practices/SOPs/standards) are mandated over the work you do? Are you in compliance with these controls? Are these controls fully implemented within your area?
- Are the risks inherent in your projects and in their deliverables identified and managed?
- Do you consciously consider and manage the risks associated with your work and how they may impact your area or other areas in the business?

Confidentiality of Risk Management Documentation

Documentation associated with the risk management process will often contain highly confidential information and must be protected as such. Such documentation may also contain information that has potential legal or regulatory implications for a company. At the outset of each project, and before creating any documentation, consideration

Copyright © 2004, Idea Group Inc. Copying or distributing in print or electronic forms without written permission of Idea Group Inc. is prohibited.

should be given to whether the particular project involves such implications and, if so, should involve appropriate personnel from other stakeholders in the organization.

People, Processes, Technology and the Hierarchy of Controls

Risk management is about risk mitigation for the most part. This may be done by reducing the impact and/or by reducing the probability of the risk occurring. To do this, various "controls" defined by a hierarchy of controls are applied. This hierarchy of controls provides a common terminology used to describe risk management. The success of risk management depends on its ability to implement changes across all of IT in the areas of policy, process, management practices, procedures and standards. To do this, establish a common understanding of how terms are used throughout the business.

There are three key elements associated with mitigating risks. Change can occur in people, processes, or technology.

- *People.* People, or more particularly their actions, can be changed in order to mitigate a risk. An example of this would be the introduction of software licence practices detailing necessary requirements for purchase and distribution of software. Employees must be made aware of the proper procedures associated with buying software and know that downloading software from the Internet constitutes inappropriate use.
- *Process.* Processes can be changed to mitigate risk. An example of this would be the introduction of access management processes (and attendant software) to reduce the risk of not properly managing access when employees leave a company.

Copyright © 2004, Idea Group Inc. Copying or distributing in print or electronic forms without written permission of Idea Group Inc. is prohibited.

Figure 1.

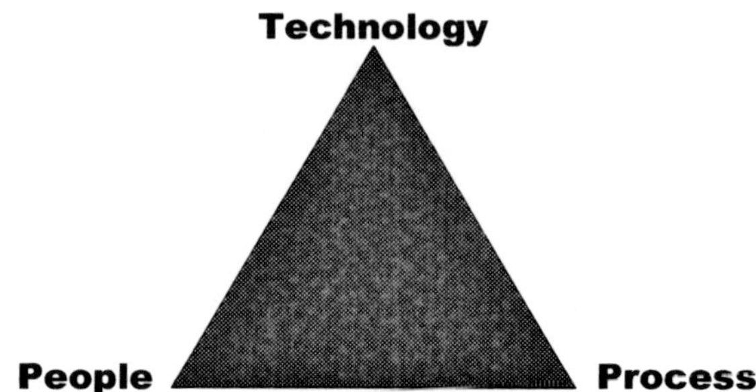

- *Technology.* Technology can be introduced or revised to ensure that a risk is mitigated. An example of this would be audit monitoring software tools on key systems and applications to preclude unauthorized access.

Hierarchy of Controls Model

Controls are frequently described as documents that foster change and are most often reflected in policy documents, also referred to as the hierarchy of controls. Having a control model provides the framework for risk mitigation by defining actions or deliverables that can be implemented to mitigate a risk. Figure 2 illustrates an example set of hierarchy of controls.

Common Terminology

The following terms describe the different controls used to mitigate risks:

Copyright © 2004, Idea Group Inc. Copying or distributing in print or electronic forms without written permission of Idea Group Inc. is prohibited.

Figure 2.

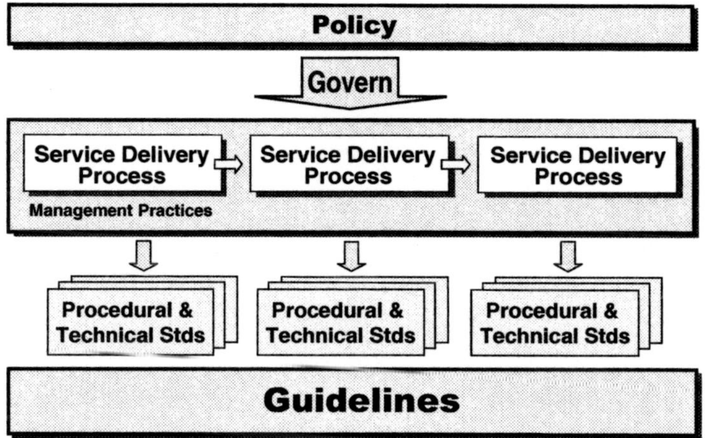

- *Policy.* Policies mandate safe and reliable working practices to ensure processes will operate to minimize risk to the business. They serve as a contract between employer and employees and are mandatory.
- *Process.* A process is 'what we do' and clearly outlines the service and targeted deliverable. A process can be described at several levels.
- *Procedural Standard.* Describes in detail how the work should be performed. Such procedural standards can be developed by an IT organization for its own use, or may be prescribed by the corporate level.
- *Technical Standard.* States what tools or rules are required to be used in executing a process or procedure. The standard may be internally or externally defined. Technical solutions would be considered to be technical standards in the hierarchy of controls.
- *Guideline.* Describes good practices for performing the process. These are not mandatory, unlike an SOP, or technical standard.

Copyright © 2004, Idea Group Inc. Copying or distributing in print or electronic forms without written permission of Idea Group Inc. is prohibited.

The Risk Management Process:

- *Risk Assessment.* Identifying risks introduced as the result of a change in the business and determining the impact of these risks, and deciding whether steps need to be taken to manage them.
- *Risk Mitigation.* Designing and implementing the controls needed to reduce the potential impact of the risk to an acceptable level.

Risk Management Model

In order to assess and mitigate risk, a standard method should be used. As stated earlier in this chapter, there is no one single risk management methodology that is better than another. The methodology below is a composite of best practices from industry and government models, most notably the National Institute of Standards and Technology and the Information Systems Audit Control Association and ISO standard 17799.

The key to success is not the model but whether the model works for your business and whether you are able as the IT risk manager to articulate the business value of having a risk management methodology. A standard methodology that all business units use to assess risk will provide the key ingredient for a successful program. The following paragraphs discuss the risk management model as shown in Figure 3, and define and explain the steps in the process.

Introduction to Key Terminology

- *Risk.* A risk is a situation or outcome that will have a negative effect. It is always associated with a negative outcome; otherwise it cannot be considered to be a risk.

Copyright © 2004, Idea Group Inc. Copying or distributing in print or electronic forms without written permission of Idea Group Inc. is prohibited.

Figure 3.

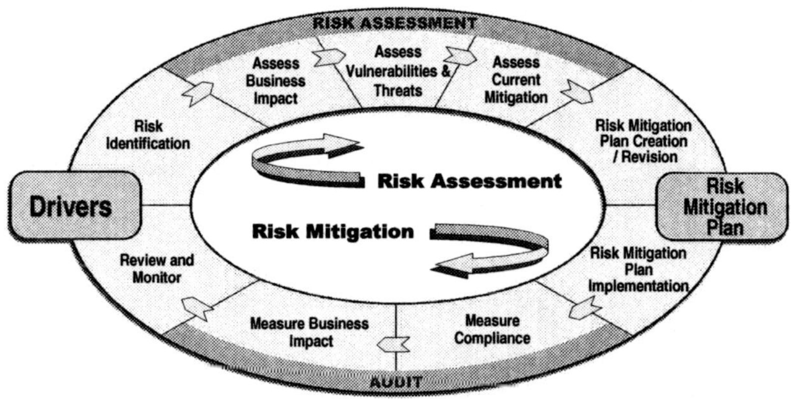

- *Source of Risk.* Source of risk is an event or circumstance that gives rise to a risk or changes the potential impact of a risk or changes the probability that a risk will occur.
- *Threat.* A threat is the potential or capacity to inflict harm. It is the person or thing that will cause the dollar impact if the risk matures.
- *Vulnerability.* A vulnerability is something inherent or intrinsic to the risk situation that introduces a weakness (i.e., "as-is" situation, a gap or weakness that makes owner susceptible to something). It has the potential to increase the probability of a risk maturing or increasing the loss or impact of a maturing risk.
- *Reward.* The positive outcome that may be acquired/achieved if a risk is taken. It makes taking the risk worthwhile and is typically the "carrot" that justifies taking the risk. The reward may or may not be guaranteed if the risk is taken. A risk jeopardizes the reward/benefit.
- *Mitigation Response.* A response to a risk where actions are taken to reduce the impact of a risk.

Copyright © 2004, Idea Group Inc. Copying or distributing in print or electronic forms without written permission of Idea Group Inc. is prohibited.

Risk Management Process Model Concepts

Some key concepts embodied within the risk management process model are worth noting:

- Risk is seldom eliminated; it is merely mitigated or controlled. As such, the risk management model is an endless loop. A risk, once mitigated, should be periodically reviewed, and controls should be tested for compliance at regular intervals.
- The essential process steps, risk assessment and risk mitigation, successively gather information that support the key steps in the overall process.

Risk Identification

The first step of the risk assessment process is the continuous monitoring required to detect changes in the environment, specifically the dynamics that may result in additional or changed risks for a company. A key step in any risk management technique is to identify the **perspective** of interest (i.e., from whose perspective should the risk scenario be analyzed — essentially, who will suffer which losses and gain which rewards?).

For some risk scenarios, it may be important to analyze the same situation from more than one **perspective** (e.g., different business units or functional areas within the company may each have a different perspective on the same risk) in order to acquire the full corporate perspective.

Copyright © 2004, Idea Group Inc. Copying or distributing in print or electronic forms without written permission of Idea Group Inc. is prohibited.

Identify Scope

Identification of scope is another key critical aspect of risk management. When conducting the risk identification process, a clear understanding of the boundaries of the analysis and the topics to be covered within the analysis should be agreed upon. What is inclusive and what is exclusive? This is particularly important when calculating the amount of loss or reward, as these will be directly affected by the amount and size of items in scope.

The scope may include technology, organizational, geographical or functional boundaries.

When analyzing key risk areas, definition of scope may be particularly important in order to work with manageable chunks of information (i.e., it may not be possible to gather data on the full impact of a regulatory law in a single risk identification session — the scope may be too large — and a decomposition of scope may be necessary). Stakeholder representatives may vary depending upon the scope of a particular assessment.

Examples of a scope statement for risk identification:

- Includes all IT systems across the enterprise *and* includes systems internal to the company as well as those managed externally by suppliers, *but* excludes process control and computer systems
- All computer systems of any type, IT, process control
- All regulated IT computer systems, for example in pharmaceutical and financial companies

Quantify Potential Reward

Each new or changed dynamic will have an associated reward. The reward can include:

Copyright © 2004, Idea Group Inc. Copying or distributing in print or electronic forms without written permission of Idea Group Inc. is prohibited.

- Anticipated revenue or sales total
- Reduction in anticipated losses
- Synergy savings
- Operating savings or cost avoidance
- Avoidance of costs due to loss of reputation
- Ability to continue with existing business practices where external circumstances may have changed

Consider both the reward **description** and the potential **value** of the reward.

Quantify Risks

To determine whether to proceed with a full risk assessment, an overview of the new or changed dynamic is required. Areas to consider include:

- The cause for the change
- The potential effect
- The rationale for the change
- Who is triggering the change

Based on an understanding of the change in dynamics, identify the potential risks to the company. These risks may be ongoing risks that have already been addressed or may be new risks. Outline both IT and business risks.

When the risks have been defined, a cursory review should be completed to determine which risks currently have been addressed and have had controls implemented through prior efforts, and which risks are new and have not been formally reviewed in the past.

Copyright © 2004, Idea Group Inc. Copying or distributing in print or electronic forms without written permission of Idea Group Inc. is prohibited.

For each risk identified, consider both the risk **description** and potential **cost** of the risk. If the risk has been previously analyzed, summarize **previous review results**.

Business Impact

The next major step involves identification of the business impact. This step involves detailed analysis of all risks identified. The objective is to assess probability and potential impact of identified risks in order to make informed decisions on appropriate next steps.

Analyze Risks

Each risk should be analyzed and classified into categories that reflect the risks to the business by type.

A sample list is below:

- Product Development and Safety
- Product Quality and Availability
- IT Systems
- Information Management
- Safeguarding Key Assets, Resources & Processes
- Sales & Marketing Practices
- Integrity of Directors & Employees
- Non-Discrimination in Employment
- Pensions
- Financial Controls
- Competition Law
- Environmental Management

Copyright © 2004, Idea Group Inc. Copying or distributing in print or electronic forms without written permission of Idea Group Inc. is prohibited.

- Employee Health & Safety
- Litigation

Quantify Current Level of Risk

A standard approach to risk quantification is shown below. This standard is based on two considerations:

1. The expected value or financial impact ($ impact) if the risk were to occur. This is always viewed from a business perspective, not a technology perspective.
2. The probability (P) or likelihood that a risk will occur.

Formula for Calculating Risk: Risk ($) = P x ($ Impact)

Risk quantification requires knowledge of the expected value of the business impact if the event occurs. The business units affected should determine the financial impact.

The **target** is the acceptable value of the measurement for this risk. Quantifying the norm provides a measure of how well the risk has been managed or mitigated at later stages within the risk management framework.

When considering the target level of risk, consider the risk reward equation (i.e., what is the acceptable level of risk that a company can accept in relation to the pursuit of the associated reward). This is the potential target level. If the current level of risk equals this target, then perhaps no mitigation is required and the company will accept this risk.

Copyright © 2004, Idea Group Inc. Copying or distributing in print or electronic forms without written permission of Idea Group Inc. is prohibited.

Assess Vulnerabilities

This assessment identifies all the components that may contribute to the actualization of the potential risk. These components are referred to as **vulnerabilities and threats**. In most cases, there will be several vulnerabilities and threats for each potential risk to the business.

Do not become wrapped up in the debate around the definitions of threats and vulnerabilities; at the end of the day it really does not matter as long as your company has a common understanding of these two terms. All too often debates over terminology drag processes down.

Identify Dimensions of Vulnerability

Those working in IT have a tendency to make judgements from a technology perspective. Often, though, it is not the technology itself that is at issue, but rather how the technology is managed, or human factors affecting the use of technology. To understand a vulnerability, the assessment process needs to determine what is putting a component at risk.

People, technology, processes, vendors, legislation, business partners, infrastructure systems, facilities, the environment, financials, and social and organizational considerations, can all be viewed as vulnerabilities. The point is to determine the most likely threats relating to the company's defined vulnerabilities. Vulnerabilities are established based on past experiences, the nature of the business, the competition, the physical location, the extent to which the business relies on technology, geographical and political considerations, and so forth.

Copyright © 2004, Idea Group Inc. Copying or distributing in print or electronic forms without written permission of Idea Group Inc. is prohibited.

Assess Mitigation Practices

The next step is to assess the mitigation strategies that are currently in place and determine what additional mitigation strategies need to be used in order to effectively manage the risks. Controls may include those that form a part of the hierarchy of controls, or they may be the result of transfer of the risk.

Typically, different vulnerabilities and threats will exist within different areas, all contributing to the risks under review. Where appropriate, the assessment of current mitigation may be undertaken by different business areas. For example, mitigating risks associated with access controls is in fact a shared responsibility between IT, business managers and human resources. The risk cannot be isolated and mitigated simply by introducing new software. A process, agreed to by all parties, must be developed and adhered to in order to ensure accesses are terminated, for example, when an individual leaves the company.

Identify Mitigation Categories

Identify the processes that are currently being used to mitigate the vulnerability or threat. Mitigation categories refer to types of controls. The most common controls are:

- Policy
- Process
- Management Practice
- Guideline
- Standard Operating Procedures (SOPs)

Copyright © 2004, Idea Group Inc. Copying or distributing in print or electronic forms without written permission of Idea Group Inc. is prohibited.

Other types include:

- Technical Standard
- Contract
- Organization/Council
- Training
- Regulation
- Software Tools

The assessment of current controls should review four key areas:

- Are there controls in place for this vulnerability or threat? (i.e., **Do they exist?**)
- **Are these controls properly implemented?** (i.e., Are they implemented everywhere they are required? Are they implemented consistently?)
- **Are the controls effective** in managing the vulnerability or threat? Have the controls been effective in the past at addressing similar potential risks? Have the potential risks been realized (i.e., have the risks previously matured) in the past?
- **Are there safeguards or compensating controls in place** to mitigate this vulnerability or threat? Have these been effective in the past?

Based on the effectiveness of existing controls and in light of the detailed review of vulnerabilities and threats, make **recommendations** on what else can be done to mitigate vulnerabilities and threats. Additional controls, new processes and/or new technology may be necessary. Obviously the final recommendations incorporated into the risk mitigation plan should present the options felt to offer the optimal "value-added" return on investment for the resources required and hence deliver the greatest impact to the business.

Copyright © 2004, Idea Group Inc. Copying or distributing in print or electronic forms without written permission of Idea Group Inc. is prohibited.

Once recommendations have been made for all risks, validate that they:

- are consistent and will address the risks
- will be acceptable to those, across all business areas, who will work with them on a day-to-day basis
- *do not* contradict existing controls or cause negative effects outside the scope
- are justified in terms of the anticipated costs, potential risk and the anticipated reward

Measure Compliance

Develop Compliance Processes, Methods and Tools

Measuring compliance is critical to the overall success of the entire risk management process. Determine if the risk management methods are actually having a positive impact and be able to measure the extent to which the mitigation controls are in fact being used. Clearly, compliance measurement is somewhat onerous; however, successful implementations depend on how easy the process is and the perception that the process is useful, and will not have a negative impact. Typically, auditors are brought in at this point in the process. The key here is to ensure that the auditors are on-board with the process and their findings will not be used against the organizations being audited. Compliance monitoring should not be viewed as the penalty phase of risk management. This is why it is so important to have a separate risk management function that is a partner with the company's audit team. Consider the following when planning compliance measurement tools:

- Scope of compliance measurement, that is, who will be measured, where and when measurements are to be taken and possibly by whom.

Copyright © 2004, Idea Group Inc. Copying or distributing in print or electronic forms without written permission of Idea Group Inc. is prohibited.

- How to perform data capture, for example, self-assessment questionnaires, Web-based tools, interviews, audit results, and metrics returned from execution of routine processes. (Do not underestimate time required to capture data.)
- How to solicit responses, for example, how to ensure responses are made to questionnaires, how to ensure data are returned as requested.
- Methods to collate and store the responses.
- Methods to measure responses, that is, determine how to use the data to measure compliance.
- Follow-up actions that may be required.
- Other information may need to be gathered in this initial planning task, including:
- inventory of what is currently under control, and
- the conflict resolution process and escalation process.

Summary

Risk management is an important corporate business process and sound management practice. Using IT risk management practices is critical to business success in the e-business age. Using a risk management framework to assess IT risks enables companies to make logical decisions about risk and helps to determine where to use resources to mitigate risks. Finally, and most importantly, using a process like the one described in this chapter does work. The key is to use the process consistently and make it part of the corporate culture.

Trusting Trusted Systems

"Who can you trust" is a popular saying in the security community, but at some point, some time, people and systems need to trust each other to

Copyright © 2004, Idea Group Inc. Copying or distributing in print or electronic forms without written permission of Idea Group Inc. is prohibited.

send and receive information, store it, use it and update it. In many cases, systems exchange critical information every few seconds (like the Wall Street markets) using a series of encryption keys or validation tokens that verify their identity to each other. Corporate e-mail systems often verify their identity to each other before replication of their contents to ensure confidential messages are not being transferred to an unauthorized server. Because of the continuously growing amounts of spam e-mail messages being sent, several proposals are being discussed to have e-mail messages "identify" themselves prior to user acceptance. Undesired (i.e., untrusted) messages would be rejected.

How does a system become "trusted"? There are usually two approaches used:

(a) The software on the system has been installed with a "known good" image that has been checked for viruses, worms, Trojan Horses and other defects that would cause it to become untrustworthy. In addition, it is loaded with special encryption or validation software that permits a valid response to security queries from systems that need to share information with it. In most cases, frequent testing of the systems security software occurs to ensure it can continue to be trusted.

(b) An independent and trusted authority, such as Etrust or Network Solutions has examined the system, and verified the organization's policies and procedures concerning the protection of customer information and their trust is serious and credible. An independent group as part of that examination may also verify the systems security software integrity.

Just as with paper documents, businesses and organizations must protect customer information to the maximum degree reasonable or practical. Information in digital format is far easier to illegally obtain, easier and faster to use for multiple purposes, and can be taken without the

Copyright © 2004, Idea Group Inc. Copying or distributing in print or electronic forms without written permission of Idea Group Inc. is prohibited.

owner's awareness, at least for some time. All of these factors — plus government regulations on customer privacy and illegal use — converge at the management level as requirements to protect customer provided information against unauthorized access and misuse.

How this task can be accomplished (or if it can be accomplished) requires the expertise of computer software experts, network administrators, facilities designers, security engineers, management and many others. Section Three of this book contains information on the various technologies and concepts available to protect data — this section describes the "why".

The simplest reason for "why" involves the expectation of trust between a customer, shareholder, supplier and the organization they provide information to. Should the trustor believe their proprietary or private information is being shared without their knowledge or approval — or has been stolen — from the trustee, they have several avenues of legal and financial redress to restore damages incurred by the breach of trust. Protection of information provided in trust for legitimate transactions bears both a risk and benefit. The risk is that it could be stolen or misused in unplanned ways, incurring legal and financial penalties. The benefits usually outweigh the risks and are derived in financial profits from increased transactions, cross-selling and up-selling opportunities, and a very low cost to service and manage the customer's account information.

Lewicki and Bunker (1996) detailed three primary forms of trust in the business marketplace:

1. *Deterrence-Based Trust:* Exists when people or organizations do what they say they would, with consistency established by a threat of punishment when performance fails. This type of trust in found in the medical, legal and financial communities when the cost of breaking that trust is so high, the cost forms deterrence against it.
2. *Knowledge-Based Trust:* Exists when the trustor can understand and predict the behavior of the other party by knowing something

Copyright © 2004, Idea Group Inc. Copying or distributing in print or electronic forms without written permission of Idea Group Inc. is prohibited.

about them, such as when agreement is reached for customized equipment or personalized jewelry.

3. *Identification-Based Trust:* Exists when similar views, beliefs, interests, goals or financial investments bind trustee and trustor. There is a common bond that is created based on knowledge about each other. An example would be membership in a political party, or in affinity credit card sponsored by a non-profit organization for its members.

Trust is broken when customer provided information is stolen, lost, corrupted, or misused. Of course, technology fails from time to time, and information is lost, usually temporarily. However, in the case of information being illegally copied, lost, exposed to the public, or misused for private benefit, management is often the first line of communication concerning questions on how such an event could have happened, and what the plans are to stop it from ever happening again.

Should a security breach occur, regardless of size or impact, a very thorough investigation and root cause analysis must be done to identify exactly what happened, why it happened, who did it, and what can be done to stop it from happening again. Executive and senior managers must be involved with these activities to understand the degree of financial, political, media and competitor risk inflicted in the organization by the breach, and how the impact can be either contained or mitigated.

As increasing amounts of business utilize the Internet, less person-to-person contact exists to actually know who is purchasing products or services. Technology now exists that emulates keystrokes and other actions that a person would normally perform, thus leading to situations where computers could "appear" to be people to other computers, based on the information sent to them. For legitimate purposes, this may be acceptable, but for illegitimate purposes such as identity theft and deliberate

Copyright © 2004, Idea Group Inc. Copying or distributing in print or electronic forms without written permission of Idea Group Inc. is prohibited.

consumer fraud, businesses could bear a tremendous financial burden that may not be covered by insurance or financial reserves.

Verifying Digital Information Outside of the Organization

As anonymous sales and transactions increase through the Internet and on-line systems, people, companies and organizations are being asked for private information concerning themselves in order to establish trust with their trading partners. In some cases, the information is reasonable and often public such as addresses, phone numbers and third-party references such as banks.

Due in large part to increases in identity theft, online fraud and online theft, system and network access is being denied to anyone unwilling to share security data to validate their identity. The Public Key Infrastructure (PKI) has been developed to share and confirm private information between two parties unwilling to share their secrets but who need to conduct business.

PKI bridges the public and private communities that demand guarantees for authenticity and non-repudiation of transactions. Trusted third parties hold the public keys used to de-encrypt messages and transactions sent with the user's private key. Similar in concept to both a customer and merchant trusting a credit card company to properly bill the customer's account and pay the merchant's account, PKI offers a stable and verifiable way for people to digitally sign documents, make large purchases and authorize medical treatments, among other uses.

The ability to share digital signatures and other files should be apparent to senior managers and executives. The savings in paper documents, waiting time and mailing fees (compared to an instant digital signature) can

Copyright © 2004, Idea Group Inc. Copying or distributing in print or electronic forms without written permission of Idea Group Inc. is prohibited.

add up to millions of dollars per year for large organizations, and can be large savings for smaller groups. PKI requires acceptance by the legal and financial communities to be fully effective, and several large corporations (such as Citibank) have started to use digital signatures where legally possible.

Summary

Security governance is a broad and deep topic requiring sustained focus on many important strategic and customer facing activities. Risk, responsibility, integrity, trust and ethics are just a few of the areas of responsibilities faced by senior management on this topic, with each requiring significant thought about assumptions, communications and responses that affect most — or all — parts of the organization.

What is interesting with all of these areas is the high degree of integration between them. In most cases, one area requires support from all of the others. Few are standalone islands, due in large part to the integration of e-mail, enterprise-wide support systems and embedded supply chains. The good news is that tremendous leverage can occur between integrated systems when implemented successfully and managed responsively.

Strong security practices can also be implemented across an organization — in most cases, incremental costs are lower than paying settlement claims and re-establishing corporate credibility after a security breach or loss.

Governance decisions set the stage for building the security architecture that leads to the selection of technology — topics that are covered in the next sections.

Copyright © 2004, Idea Group Inc. Copying or distributing in print or electronic forms without written permission of Idea Group Inc. is prohibited.

Best Practices Framework

Best Practice	*Criticality*	*Frequency*	*Participants*	*Activity Results*
Is access to specific information limited to people who need to know or use it?	High	Quarterly	Management, security	Direct linkage of information to people based on business need
Have security assumptions at all levels of the organization been verified? Are they linked to business need?	High	Six months	Management, security, finance, marketing	Integrated security plan based on business need and investment availability
Does the organization adhere to best practices in responsibility, integrity, trust and ethics?	High	Six months	Management, security, finance, human resources	Public and employee trust resulting in higher revenues and market share
Does the organization have reasonable policies in place for employee monitoring and privacy? Are they written?	High	Six months	Management, security	Reduced confusion about what is private and not private at work
Are plans in place to communicate good and bad news with customers and shareholders?	Medium	Quarterly	Management, finance	Confidence in management ability to accomplish goals and manage problems
Are effective safeguards in place to protect customer information?	High	Quarterly	Management, sales, marketing	Few customer complaints about improper disclosures of private information
Have the risk assumptions for the organization been confirmed? Are they still accurate?	High	Six months	Management, security, finance	Lowered risk levels due to accurate analysis and avoidance planning
Are risk compliance tools in place and are they being used?			Management, security, finance	Predictable, reliable processes to determine and reduce risk

Copyright © 2004, Idea Group Inc. Copying or distributing in print or electronic forms without written permission of Idea Group Inc. is prohibited.

Section II
Architecture Issues

This section is focused on building the information security architecture, including the issues of what is important for executives and senior managers to consider about how to align the security, application and infrastructure architectures for maximum benefit. Additional discussion is provided concerning the construction of multiple protection barriers, determining internal security threats and performing disaster planning in worst-case scenarios.

Unfortunately, there is no boilerplate information security architecture plan that can be scaled up or down to meet the needs of every organization. Each organization has different information security requirements, unique financial constraints and individual risk tolerances and technical resources. A small e-commerce company may create a security plan that costs a million dollars that meets their needs, while a large government agency may spend $100 million and believe substantial security deficiencies remain to be remedied. Balancing these factors with customer and shareholder expectations is a difficult job, and all of these factors change frequently, often every day, as new threats become visible. However, it is clear that some commonalities do exist across most IT organizations, permitting leveraging of Best Practices frameworks.

Copyright © 2004, Idea Group Inc. Copying or distributing in print or electronic forms without written permission of Idea Group Inc. is prohibited.

Security architectures are often created in response to a known threat or anticipated situation. In most cases, proactive thinking across a wide spectrum of possible risks and threats is usually more cost effective than creating and applying single solutions that do not directly address collateral impacts or opportunities. The cost effectiveness comes from leveraging many points of security — firewalls, updated OS patches, audit trails, role-based access, multi-level management access approvals, automated virus installations, etc. — which can leverage each other to isolate and contain security brecches. The single point approach may be cheaper initially, but much more expensive should a number of different single point approaches be required to address multi-pronged types of attacks — which is becoming more of the norm.

The Microsoft Exchange virus and worm attacks of the past four years indicates that having an adaptable, leveragable and agile security response capability was more effective than applying a monolithic or proprietary approach. Organizations that had single point security technologies or processes had to constantly replan their processes and technical staff to counter previously unknown threats and attacks that a single approach could not contain.

The first step in building a strong defense is to identify possible threats, their sources, and overall impact to the organization – items found in the threat matrix model.

Copyright © 2004, Idea Group Inc. Copying or distributing in print or electronic forms without written permission of Idea Group Inc. is prohibited.

Chapter V

Architecture Issues

Lawrence M. Oliva

Introduction

This chapter is focused on building the information architecture: what is important to consider, how to align the security, application and infrastructure architectures for maximum benefit, constructing multiple protection barriers, determining internal security threats and performing disaster planning in worst case scenarios.

Every organization has different information security, different financial resources and different risk tolerances. Balancing all of these factors with customer and shareholder expectations is a difficult job, and all of these factors change frequently. However, it is clear that some commonalities do exist across most IT organizations, permitting leveraging of best practices frameworks.

Security architectures are often created in response to a known threat or anticipated situation. While a valid activity, proactive thinking is often more cost effective than single solutions that do not directly address collateral impacts or opportunities.

Copyright © 2004, Idea Group Inc. Copying or distributing in print or electronic forms without written permission of Idea Group Inc. is prohibited.

Building a Threat Matrix

Every organization should build a threat matrix as a way to identify, prepare for, and manage security risks. It can be simple or complex, but just having it and using it as a preparation device will help immensely should a serious problem occur. A standard model might look like this:

	Source of Threat	*Response Time*	*Impact Value*
External	Hacker	Immediate	High
Internal	Employee	Immediate	High
Unknown	Terrorist	Immediate	High
Financial Fraud	Customer	Immediate	Low to High
Access Denial	Multiple	Immediate	High
Sabotage	Multiple	Depends on type	Low to High

Senior management must participate in these discussions and decisions to help balance cost and risk trade-off decisions often made by technical staff that may not have a "big-picture" organization perspective in mind. Often, cost trade-offs are made that protect the group paying for the improvements, but leave other groups open to a slower recovery, or in some cases being even more exposed than before, as protection they thought they had no longer exists.

Each plan must be adapted to the specific needs of the IT organization, its shareholders, customers and suppliers. A hospital would have a very different plan than a newspaper, for example. A chemical factory would have a different plan than a city government.

A superior threat matrix plan comes from identifying as many vulnerabilities as possible so they can be addressed and reduced in risk. Threat countermeasures containing technical, policy and process elements are also a critical part of the matrix that requires executive participation and support. Determining the degree of risk to absorb and mitigate through investment are often difficult to make. In either case, the organization may incur a very costly bill with little advantage to customers or shareholders

Copyright © 2004, Idea Group Inc. Copying or distributing in print or electronic forms without written permission of Idea Group Inc. is prohibited.

other than business continuity at the previous pace. While remaining in business is not entirely negative, not being able to produce a profit may be too large an obstacle to overcome, should the impact exceed estimates.

Aligning Architectures to Service Level Agreements

Service Level Agreements (SLAs) are usually contractual documents that specify minimum levels of professional service delivery, computer and network availability time, capacity and performance levels, security access protocols and other areas of interest to customers and suppliers obligated to adhere to them.

In most situations, customers paying for the services and access expect 24×7, 99.999% system uptime, with the supplier hoping for less stringent performance metrics, especially if financial penalties are incurred for non-performance.

Although there are several approaches to take to support SLAs with high performance levels, most security and computer experts would agree that the simplest and least expensive approach involves aligning the computer, network and security architectures into a common infrastructure. Integrating these as a common infrastructure foundation permits significant leverage of equipment and personnel and provides greater operational control of organizations' computing operations.

Other advantages of architectural alignment include:

- Standardized security processes and equipment
- Limited external access points that can be monitored for unauthorized intrusion
- Reduced costs due to fewer hardware and software components
- Reduced training levels for support staff (due to standardized equipment)

Copyright © 2004, Idea Group Inc. Copying or distributing in print or electronic forms without written permission of Idea Group Inc. is prohibited.

- Ability to quickly diagnosis and resolve problems, as problems often occur in the same systems, and one fix may correct other problems triggered by that one defect
- Tuning of components for maximum performance is enhanced through a common architecture that has fewer "friction points" (i.e., discrete software components from different suppliers, different networks with unique firewall configurations, and data sets that require constant reformatting and normalizing)
- The time to integrate new applications and technologies onto a standardized platform is greatly reduced by having a common set of software interfaces, security access points and performance monitors already in place

From the executive management perspective, service level agreements are excellent documents to have in place, as they do stipulate some level of performance. However, the expense of "five nines" uptime (99.999) may exceed the organization's budget. The customer cost of managing the SLA itself—with frequent management meetings to discuss issues, continuous collection of system metrics, escalation of financial penalties perceived to be incorrect, and discussions about who or what caused problems to occur — is often overlooked during contractual negotiations. For a large organization with a "five nines" SLA level, the management costs are often $250,000 per year, including executive time. Ways to reduce this cost include:

- Lowering the SLA level to 99.99% or 99.9% performance level—moving from a 99.99% uptime level to a 99.9% uptime level is a difference of 7.7 more hours per year (to a total of 8.8 hours) on a 24×7 basis;
- Prioritizing on "what must be 99.999% up" such as network firewalls and security systems, and what can be off-line for eight to 10 hours per year for maintenance, such as storage and mainframe access; and

Copyright © 2004, Idea Group Inc. Copying or distributing in print or electronic forms without written permission of Idea Group Inc. is prohibited.

- Writing SLAs that can be "flexed" or changed depending on the needs of the business or organization. For example, retail businesses typically need 100% data processing uptime during the Christmas season, but may be able to accommodate (and pay for) a 99.9% uptime SLA the remainder of the year.

System Availability Uptime Percentages	Hours Per Year
100% (24 x 7)	8760
99.999%	8759.9
99.99%	8759.1
99.9%	8751.2
99.0%	8672.4

Constructing Multi-Layer Protection Barriers

The most effective security systems are architected and deployed in multiple layers to create a sustainable barrier against multiple, and different, types of attacks. For large organizations with multiple public Web portals, employee dial-in access points and supplier support networks, developing a multi-level barrier usually requires a multimillion dollar engineering, purchase, deployment and operational investment.

Typical technical approaches to building a multi-level security system involve:

- A foundation level that requires the user to have a minimal level of security to access (even a publicly known and shared password)
- A second tier that identifies and validates the computer or terminal they are using to the network (through a cookie or ID token)
- A third tier that limits access to "known" users (users that can provide some type of authentication that has not been shared with other people)

Copyright © 2004, Idea Group Inc. Copying or distributing in print or electronic forms without written permission of Idea Group Inc. is prohibited.

- A fourth tier that further limits access computer and user access without correct responses to a computer and user "challenge question" that only that computer and user would have. The computer could provide an encrypted key that was sent to it the last time it was connected to the network, and the user would be asked what their last password was.
- A fifth tier requires a biometric identifier from the user, such as their fingerprint, voiceprint, faceprint, retinal scan or signature sample. One — or a combination of two — of these factors would provide a very high level of confidence that the person logging in really was the correct person.

From a senior management perspective, all of this security costs a lot of money with little visible benefit or tangible return to the organization. However, the cost of not protecting information assets, systems and networks from malicious attack can be extraordinary as calculated by different private and government organizations (in the summer of 2003, private businesses suffered a loss of over $3.5 billion dollars recovering from worms and viruses [CERT, 2003]). Even if the calculations are off by a factor of five (i.e., are 20% correct) it is clear that the cumulative financial costs are very, very large.

So how does all of this information tie back to building multi-level barriers? Each organization must examine the value of its information assets and systems and determine how much investment is reasonable to protect it. For a small organization, the investment threshold may be very low, and dependent upon outsource suppliers to provide virus and worm network filters, combined with one or two levels of user identification verification.

For a medium to large organization that has hundreds or thousands of computers and users, calculating how many, and what type of barriers and fallback systems should be purchased can take several months and a team

Copyright © 2004, Idea Group Inc. Copying or distributing in print or electronic forms without written permission of Idea Group Inc. is prohibited.

of dedicated security experts looking at the existing equipment and user policies. Once the costs have been identified, senior managers and executives can make a business decision on the costs, schedules, policies and enforcement mechanisms that make sense for their information assets, employees, customers, suppliers and shareholders.

Revealing Internal Threats to IT Security Processes

Virtually all security surveys indicate the greatest threat to the security of information assets comes from within the organization. Computer hardware engineers have developed technology that permits users and systems to transfer and save massive amounts of information quickly, easily, and cheaply. In many cases, there is no record (also called a "logfile") that a copy or transfer has ever been made to the user's system or storage device, such as a flash memory device or CDROM. In just a few minutes, copies of an organization's payroll, customer or patient files, and core technology information assets can be copied off and taken out of the building. If an insider gains access to files through a network connection, the information could be downloaded to another computer 10,000 miles away.

How can potential internal threats be identified and nullified without implementing draconian access methods that reduce user productivity and decrease employee morale?

First, ensure a written policy is in place that details management expectations concerning the business and personal use of information systems and networks. One of the key points should prohibit the sharing of user passwords or authentication tokens between users. The policy should have formal penalties for misuse of the organization's systems and information assets.

Copyright © 2004, Idea Group Inc. Copying or distributing in print or electronic forms without written permission of Idea Group Inc. is prohibited.

Second, have all employees acknowledge they have received a copy of the policy — this can be done through e-mail or a Web-enabled data collection tool.

Third, for the most critical information assets and databases, have technical and security engineers activate system audit-logging capabilities so that a record is created by the computer system about who logs onto critical information systems and databases, and for how long. This information should be compared against a list of users who absolutely must have access. All others should be removed from the access lists.

Fourth, as part of the network monitoring activities, security engineers should watch for unusual large file transfers inside the organization's firewalls. In many cases, large files are routinely transmitted on standard schedule. Examples of these types of files include account records, financial files, supplier inventory records and digital images. The engineers can quickly identify the owners of most of these files, and verify their legitimacy. All other files should be examined closely for transmission purpose, valid ownership and appropriate storage method. For example, a mainframe sending a 50-megabyte quarterly financial statement to the CFO's laptop computer on the last day of each quarter is a reasonable situation. However, a marketing computer sending a 100-megabyte file with customer account names and purchasing histories to a desktop computer at an employee's home office just one time in the past 10 years may warrant a second look.

Although most information theft does occur internally, the vast majority of employees are honest and do their best to protect company information. Given the damage that just one security breach can have on an organization's reputation (such as TriWest Healthcare Alliance, Gehrke, 2003) and products (such as the posting of some of Microsoft's Windows 2000 and NT4.0 source code on the Internet in February 2004, Musgrove, 2004) it makes sense for senior managers and executives to limit the

Copyright © 2004, Idea Group Inc. Copying or distributing in print or electronic forms without written permission of Idea Group Inc. is prohibited.

opportunity for theft to occur. Ensuring the right people have the correct access to the information they need to do their work, and then verifying unusual situations—that may be entirely legitimate—helps reduce the risk of unknown theft or misuse occurring.

Is Disaster Recovery Planning Important?

Yes, for continuity of business operations after a major unplanned event impacts primary computing or network operations. Being able to continue revenue producing or customer facing operations is often a mission critical objective for both the organization and its customers. Without a formal plan in place during a time of crisis and chaos, the recovery of business operations to a normal level will take much longer and cost much more than anticipated. This is due in large part to logistics and communication with suppliers and partners, waiting for equipment and resources required to arrive to help, and developing a recovery plan based on incomplete or unrealistic assumptions or information.

In most cases, disaster planning often leverages existing equipment and capabilities to minimize investment expense. Recovery equipment and systems are shared with production systems to reduce the time required to implement them during an emergency, as well as activating security policies and procedures required to operate effectively.

Security processes are part of the recovery planning efforts. Transferring customer records, supplier records or proprietary information must occur without error to avoid interruption to business processes or a loss of trust during an unusual event. Plans and training activities need to be prepared to accommodate plausible situations, with rehearsals for all participants to determine weak points that require improvement and investment.

Copyright © 2004, Idea Group Inc. Copying or distributing in print or electronic forms without written permission of Idea Group Inc. is prohibited.

Senior managers need to participate in these planning sessions and rehearsal activities to provide suggestions, critique and visibility to all members of the security and recovery teams. Understanding the "big-picture" impact and investment provides a perspective different than a pure technical or operational focus, often leading to improvements that would otherwise be overlooked.

Disaster planning is a very serious and expensive process. It assumes very difficult scenarios will occur that require the same four basic management skills mentioned earlier in this section—responsibility, integrity, trust and ethics — to successfully execute.

Summary

Security architectures must focus on business threats, operational continuity, and recovery activities. In many cases, they begin to implement or expand the overall themes described in the governance planning activities detailed in the previous section. In addition to defining and engineering system redundancy, operational flexibility and a strong infrastructure to build upon, security architectures focus on the business requirements that must be supported.

Weaving together multiple threads of process, resources and technology, security planners span the "what if" world to the "how" world within the confines of budget, schedule and technical capability. Given the uncertainty of the type of threats, where they might come from, and what impact they might cause, some might say the planning challenge is overwhelming. In some cases it is, which requires a return to the underlying assumptions and objectives to revalidate them. In other cases, significant thought and cross-organizational planning become the only way to successfully overcome the challenges.

Copyright © 2004, Idea Group Inc. Copying or distributing in print or electronic forms without written permission of Idea Group Inc. is prohibited.

Best Practices Framework

Best Practice	Criticality	Frequency	Participants	Activity Results
Review and verify the current threat matrix against current assumptions	High	Six months	Management, security	Current and accurate threat matrix to proactively plan responses against
Verify all architectures are aligned against current SLAs	Medium	Six months	Management, security, IT operations, finance	Maximum leverage of IT resources and operations
Review current security barriers to ensure they provide reasonable protection against newly defined risks	High	Quarterly	Management, security, IT operations	Defensible security practices and procedures against current risks
Review all processes concerning the protection of IT resources from internal attack or loss	High	Quarterly	Management, security, IT operations,	Reduced risk or loss from internal attack
Review and verify all disaster recovery plans are current and deployable	High	Six months	Management, security, IT operations, finance	Achievable and deployable disaster recovery plan that reduces impact to employees, customers, shareholders and management

Copyright © 2004, Idea Group Inc. Copying or distributing in print or electronic forms without written permission of Idea Group Inc. is prohibited.

Section III

Technology Issues

Section Overview

This section reviews several information security technologies that are critical to just about every organization that has information systems. Written for executives and senior managers who are aware of some of the technology components — but who are not experts — overviews about protecting computer operating systems, wireless local area networks (LANs), data obsolescence, data recovery, public key infrastructure, biometrics and smartcards are provided.

The objective is to expose technologies that are close to full market acceptance and introduction, and that are useful to security engineers, senior managers and executives as they prepare budgets and resource plans.

Overall Strategy

Given the multiple methods, technologies and objectives applied by hackers, crackers, teenagers and employees to gain unauthorized access

Copyright © 2004, Idea Group Inc. Copying or distributing in print or electronic forms without written permission of Idea Group Inc. is prohibited.

to information assets, the management strategy to defeat their efforts also requires a multi-faceted approach. As an omnipresent enabler, technology plays a key role in automatically closing, sensing, locating, identifying and documenting intrusive and unapproved access to information systems and networks.

When properly selected, installed and configured, technology systems provide 24×7 support to security experts and engineers who can provide the necessary analysis and final decisions concerning intrusions, equipment failure, software error, or planned security testing. In general, technology security barriers are grouped into:

- *Infrastructure Protection:* provides a base-level foundation upon which enables higher levels of security to successfully inter-operate and communicate successfully
- *Operating System and Application Software Protection:* Securing or isolating thc opcrating and application software against authorized changes and modifications by removing unused software components and requiring that all changes be made by the system administrator under configuration management processes
- *Hardware Verification:* provides an irrefutable identity code embedded in hardware that is not easily or cheaply changed and can be used for auditing and user verification purposes
- *Planning and Managing Data Obsolescence:* ensures that data collected and stored over many years time can be successfully recovered and utilized despite changes in technical standards and performance
- *Backup and Recovery Protocols:* enables the accurate duplication and recovery of information currently used by the organization, should a non-recoverable hardware failure occur
- *Authorized System Access Methods:* provides various levels of authentication support to ensure that only authorized people and systems can gain access to information and networks

Copyright © 2004, Idea Group Inc. Copying or distributing in print or electronic forms without written permission of Idea Group Inc. is prohibited.

- *Security System Verification:* verifies that the security systems are working as planned, in accordance with generally accepted industry standards, policies and practices

Applied together with a solid architecture and governance foundation, equipment and software provide substantial protection from multiple threats inside and outside the organization. Of course, there is no "perfect" security solution — the computing and communications markets are too innovative, dynamic and market driven to agree on the rigid standards that type of draconian approach would require.

Infrastructure Protection

The computing infrastructure for most organizations provides the "dial tone" services, including network operations, telecom and data transport, system integration of commercial-off-the-shelf (COTS) software, Domain Name Services (DNS), enterprise directory services (single password across all systems) and ongoing support operations. Protection of the infrastructure involves physical security of data center computing equipment, data libraries and tape or disk backups, and redundant network access points to avoid single points of failure. In addition, redundant power sources are available and hardened (protected) to ensure continuity of operations in case of commercial power outages due to power grid failure or weather related problems.

Protecting the physical infrastructure is a traditional IT activity that has been successfully accomplished — there are very few reports about data centers being physically attacked by terrorists or intruders, and even fewer reports of any physical thefts occurring. Staff members, according to published reports, have caused virtually all thefts from inside data centers.

Copyright © 2004, Idea Group Inc. Copying or distributing in print or electronic forms without written permission of Idea Group Inc. is prohibited.

Chapter VI

Wireless Information Security

Clifton Poole
National Defense University, USA

Introduction

The proliferation of wireless local area networks in the enterprise and home domains has increased dramatically within the past several years as the 802.11b protocol has emerged as the standard of choice for wireless communication (Al-Saleh, 2002). A host of wireless networking products is now available to complete your home or enterprise wireless network. Since 2001, the product selection for the home user has multiplied ten-fold since that time. There are entire sections of the consumer electronics dedicated to the sale of products for the small office/home office (SOHO).

Many corporations are now using wireless LANs as their preferred access methods within their facilities because of the solutions' ease of installation, reduced maintenance with moves and changes, and flexibility of deployment (Al-Saleh, 2002). Changing a network using wireless technology requires fewer modifications to the physical environment. By using wireless devices to build a network, a forklift upgrade—an upgrade to a computer network or other electronic system that requires a massive hardware investment—is greatly reduced. Wireless LANs also allow a

Copyright © 2004, Idea Group Inc. Copying or distributing in print or electronic forms without written permission of Idea Group Inc. is prohibited.

user with a laptop the freedom to roam about his or her enterprise and still maintain access to the Internet and the rest of the network. The wireless solution is more elegant than running Ethernet when the computers are far apart from each other and users are still required to have access.

Private and open wireless LAN (WLAN) are the two types of networks available to the wireless user. Most WLANs are visible to users and require varying degrees of authentication to gain access. Private WLANs are usually associated with large enterprises and have a configuration that requires users to authenticate onto the network. A shared key authentication model allows users access and limits the number of connections for the enterprise. Many SOHO implementations are moving to this model because it affords them a higher level of assurance of their data. The open system authentication model requires no authentication to gain access to the network. The network owner is allowing any user in range of the signal to connect to the network available resources. In most cases that is as simple as a high bandwidth connection to the Internet. There are many networks that unknowingly give users access to shared resources because access points are improperly configured or managed.

The sheer volume of products and terms makes it difficult to understand what wireless is and how it will change your view of networking. This chapter highlights the characteristics, complexities and culture surrounding the 802.11b protocol. Here are a few wireless terms explaining how WLAN operates, some unusual and future practices in WLAN, and WLAN vulnerabilities and WLAN security strategies.

Definitions

802.11b is an extension to 802.11 that applies to wireless LANs and provides 11 megabits per second transmission in the 2.4 gigahertz band. 802.11b standard allows wireless functionality comparable to Ethernet.

Copyright © 2004, Idea Group Inc. Copying or distributing in print or electronic forms without written permission of Idea Group Inc. is prohibited.

802.11 is a family of specifications developed by the Institute of Electrical and Electronics Engineers (IEEE) for wireless LAN technology.

- *Access point* is a hardware device or a computer's software that acts as a communication hub for users of a wireless device to connect to a wired LAN. Access points are important for providing heightened wireless security and for extending the physical range of service for a wireless user. This is sometimes called a wireless "hot spot".
- *SSID* (Service Set Identifier) is the unique identifier assigned to all the access points in a WLAN. The 32-character name acts as a password when a mobile device tries to connect to the access point. The different names prevent unauthorized users from accessing a network.
- *WEP* (Wired Equivalent Privacy) is a security protocol for wireless local area networks defined in the 802.1 lb standard. WEP is used at the two lowest layers of the OSI model — the data link and physical layers; it therefore does not offer end-to-end security. WEP aims to provide security by encrypting data over radio waves so that it is protected as it is transmitted from one end point to another.
- *Wi-Fi* is short for wireless fidelity and is another name for IEEE 802.11b. It is a trade term promulgated by the Wireless Ethernet Compatibility Alliance. "Wi-Fi" is used in place of 802.11b in the same way that Ethernet is used in place of IEEE 802.3.
- *WLAN* (wireless local area network) is a type of local-area network that uses high-frequency radio waves rather than wires to communicate between nodes. You will find WLAN networks configured for private use within business and home settings or as public WLANs or Wi-Fi networks.
- *WPA* (Wi-Fi Protected Access) is a specification of standards-based, interoperable security enhancements that strongly increase the level of data protection and access control for existing and future wireless LAN systems. WPA was constructed to provide an im-

Copyright © 2004, Idea Group Inc. Copying or distributing in print or electronic forms without written permission of Idea Group Inc. is prohibited.

proved data encryption and to provide user authentication (Wi-Fi, 2003).

How Does Wireless LAN Work?

The 802.11b standard defines two modes: infrastructure mode and ad hoc mode. In infrastructure mode, the wireless network consists of at least one access point connected to the wired network infrastructure and a set of wireless end stations. This configuration is called a Basic Service Set (BSS) and each BSS has a SSID. An Extended Service Set (ESS) is a set of two or more BSSs forming a single subnetwork that share an SSID. Since most corporate WLANs require access to the wired LAN for services (file servers, printers, Internet links), they will operate in infrastructure mode. Access points typically cover a range of 300 to 500 feet. The number of access points for configuration of a WLAN in infrastructure mode varies depending on the size of the physical area requiring coverage, network configuration, physical limitation of the coverage areas and the number of users per segment.

Ad hoc mode (also called peer-to-peer mode or an Independent Basic Service Set, or IBSS) is simply a set of 802.11 wireless stations that

Figure 1. Basic and Extended Service Sets

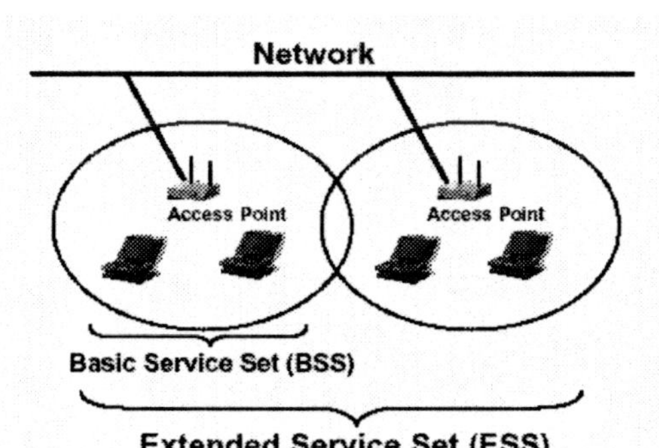

Copyright © 2004, Idea Group Inc. Copying or distributing in print or electronic forms without written permission of Idea Group Inc. is prohibited.

Figure 2. Notional Wireless Network

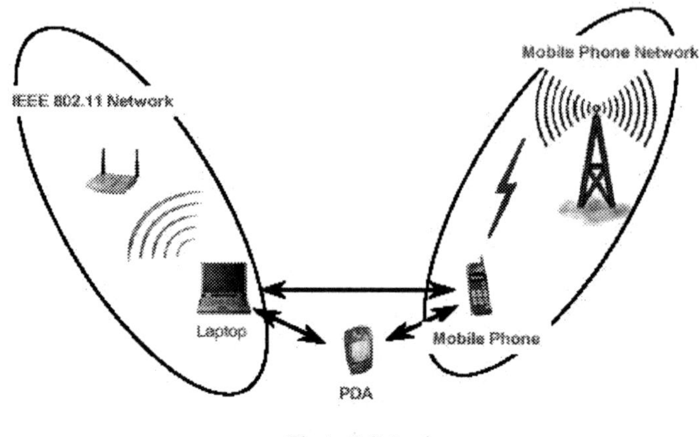

communicate directly with one another without using an access point or any connection to a wired network. This mode is useful for quickly and easily setting up a wireless network anywhere that a wireless infrastructure does not exist or is not required for services, such as a classroom, meeting area, or airport, or where access to the wired network is barred (such as for consultants at a client site). In a classroom setting, the IBSS works well for sharing files with members of a project team or submitting completed work to a central folder on an instructor's computer.

To take advantage of the 802.11b in either mode you have to have a wireless network interface card (NIC) installed in your device. The NIC is installed in an available PCMCIA slot and configured for use within the WLAN. Newer computers come with Wi-Fi capability as a part of the standard configuration and do not require a NIC.

Users become members of WLAN by means of authentication. The 802.11b protocol has two means to authenticate users: open system authentication and shared key authentication.

Copyright © 2004, Idea Group Inc. Copying or distributing in print or electronic forms without written permission of Idea Group Inc. is prohibited.

There is no authentication required to become a member of a WLAN that is set up as an open system. The client simply responds with a MAC address to gain access. The client, without any true means to authenticate, must trust that it is communicating with an actual access point. Often, clients are not granted access because the SSID is not known or passed properly from the access point. It is important to know the unique identifier in order to ensure access. With most applications this handshake is accomplished automatically and unbeknownst to the user.

In shared key authentication, a challenge-response technique is used to grant access to the WLAN. Karygiannis and Owens (2002) explain that the client, using a cryptographic key that is shared with the access point, encrypts the challenge and returns the result to the access point. The access point decrypts the result computed by the client and allows access only if the decrypted value is the same as the random challenge transmitted. This authentication method is a rudimentary cryptographic technique, and it does not provide mutual authentication. That is, the client does not authenticate the AP, and therefore there is no assurance that a client is communicating with a legitimate AP and wireless network. This is seen as a disadvantage of the current wireless implementation.

Figure 3. Challenge and Response Handshake

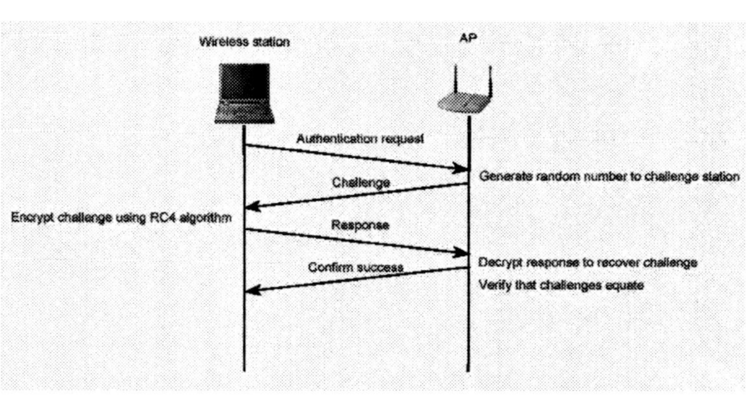

Copyright © 2004, Idea Group Inc. Copying or distributing in print or electronic forms without written permission of Idea Group Inc. is prohibited.

Security is the number one disadvantage of installing a WLAN. Often stated as the "wild, wild west" of networking, WLANs offer numerous opportunities for intruders to infiltrate the enterprise. Establishing a WLAN is like placing a piece of network cable out of your window with a sign that says "free Internet connection". People may want to test the line to see if it is active. Once they find activity on the line they will try to expand their access and privilege as far as the wired LAN's security allows. The disadvantages are overshadowed by the distinct advantages offered by installing a WLAN.

The advantages are:

- *Mobility:* Users not tied down to one location and are able to access files, network resources, and the Internet without having to physically connect to the network with wires.
- *Increased Productivity:* Users of mobile devices work more for the corporation when they are not physically in the building. You will find mobile users in trains, planes, buses and cars working with their mobile device. Some users are more productive once they move outside the confined spaces of the office and into more comfortable common areas.
- *Rapid Installation:* The effort required for installation is reduced because network connections are made almost immediately. No walls are removed, no one is sent into the floors or ceiling to pull wire and no modifications have to be made to the wiring closet.
- *Flexibility:* Users can quickly install a small WLAN for temporary needs such as a classroom, conference and other temporary venues.
- *Scalability:* WLAN network topologies can easily be configured to meet specific application and installation needs and to scale from small peer-to-peer networks to very large enterprise networks that enable roaming over a broad area.

Copyright © 2004, Idea Group Inc. Copying or distributing in print or electronic forms without written permission of Idea Group Inc. is prohibited.

Wireless Practices

Hackers are spending a good amount of time exploiting wireless networks. Hackers began "war dialing" — dialing phone numbers until they found an open modem — to access networks. The 1990s Internet boom created easier and more direct avenues of attack, such as Internet Protocol scanners and packet sniffers. LANs are inherently more secure than WLANs because LANs are somewhat protected by the physical aspects of their structure, having some or all parts of the network inside a building that can be protected from unauthorized access. WLANs, which are over radio waves, do not have the same physical structure and therefore are more vulnerable to tampering. The configuration of the 802.11b protocol allows ease of access to all trusted and not-so-trusted users. This openness has created the next generation of network intrusion: "war driving".

War driving is using a laptop's wireless NIC set in a promiscuous mode to pick up unsecured WLAN signals. At this stage of the game, hackers are war driving around seeking — or "LAN-jacking", as it is sometimes called — wireless networks for anonymous and free high-speed Internet access. Wireless LAN war drivers routinely drive in their cars equipped with laptops loaded with a wireless LAN card, an external high-gain antenna and a global positioning system receiver. The wireless LAN card and GPS receiver feed signals into freeware, such as NetStumbler, to detect access points and their identifiers along with their GPS-derived locations. A permutation of war driving is war flying, where the vehicle is a plane instead of a car. In academic settings, students have been known to walk with laptops enabled with scanning software to locate access points in buildings. The activity of locating access points has really taken off in the past few years.

To mark AP locations, hackers use a technique called war chalking (*www.warchalking.org*). They simply use chalk to place a special symbol

Copyright © 2004, Idea Group Inc. Copying or distributing in print or electronic forms without written permission of Idea Group Inc. is prohibited.

on a sidewalk or other surface that indicates a nearby wireless network, especially one that offers Internet access. War driving and war chalking are activities that can be thought of as counter-cultural since the intended audience may not be the owner of the network that is targeted. Over the past couple of years many people have come together to support a global war-driving day when all the individual participants provide the data from the war driving experience to a central database. This is an idea with great commercial promise. Many mainstream retailers (including Starbucks Coffee and Kinko's) have witnessed the appeal of wireless devices and have embraced the newest trend — hotspots.

Trends

Hotspots are 802.11b-compliant public network nodes available to wireless users that are often located in heavily populated places such as airports, train stations, shops, marinas, conventions centers and hotels. Hotspots typically have a short range of access and are oriented on a specific geographic location. There are thousands of these locations that offer free or low-cost wireless access to the Internet and network

Figure 4. War Chalking Symbols Card (http://www.warchalking.org/story/2002/8/20/17730/3808)

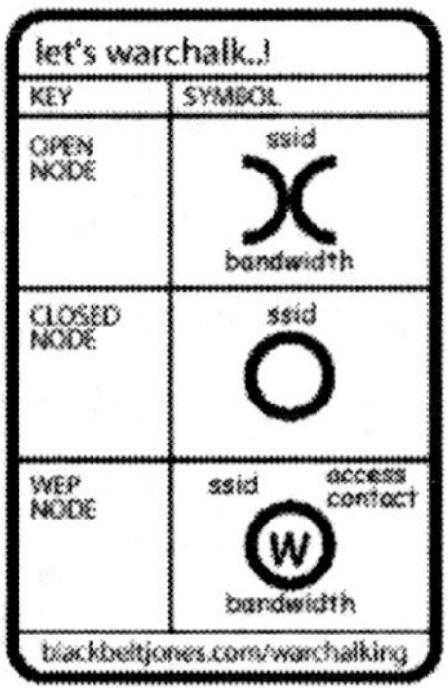

Copyright © 2004, Idea Group Inc. Copying or distributing in print or electronic forms without written permission of Idea Group Inc. is prohibited.

resources. Hotspot will change our culture by providing high-speed Internet access anywhere and at all the times.

Many retailers have made the business decision to install hotspots to increase sales of their products. National and international hotels, bakeries and coffee houses use the free access to attract customers in the hopes that more coffee and pastries are sold as users access high speed connection points. Users have ready access to the outside and with virtual private network connections, and can easily reach back to the office to retrieve content from the corporate network. The use of hotspots has created a new culture of users who think wireless access should be open and free.

Organizations such as Community Wireless and its Community Wireless Networking Project partners plan to provide free wireless access to all (*http://www.communitywireless.org/*). Using commercial off the shelf and license-free WLAN technology (802.11), various groups and individuals are embracing bandwidth and content, and sharing it with their community. There are projects partners across the globe that have realized that wireless networking is for the masses and they hope to attract business community support on the idea.

Vulnerabilities

All the vulnerabilities that exist in a conventional wired LAN apply to wireless technologies (Karygiannis & Owens, 2002). Managers must prepare to remedy the WLAN vulnerabilities — weaknesses in the configuration, implementation, design or management of a network or system — with greater vigilance. Wireless networks present unique challenges when trying to mitigate threats — anything that can disrupt the proper functioning of a network or system. The wireless devices bring to the table more problems because of their mobile nature. They move from network to network, gaining connection to the Internet and returning to the

Copyright © 2004, Idea Group Inc. Copying or distributing in print or electronic forms without written permission of Idea Group Inc. is prohibited.

Figure 5. 802.11b Wireless Security

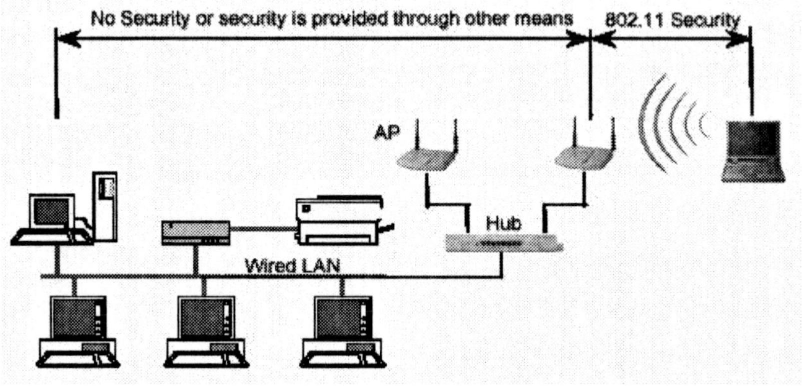

corporate WLAN with the possibility of carrying all sorts of malicious code. In a sense, mobile users should be thought of as a "malicious code carrier" and immediately quarantined in the demilitarized zone until they receive proper scanning to remove all know malware (malicious software). Users can inadvertently carry malware and infect the corporate LAN if they have not taken the proper precautions.

The NIST Special Publication 800-48 identifies some of the most prevalent threats and vulnerabilities to wireless devices. They are organized to illustrate which information assurance principle is violated when not properly mitigated.

Confidentiality violations occur if:

- Sensitive information that is not encrypted (or is encrypted with weak cryptographic techniques) and that is transmitted between two wireless devices may be intercepted and disclosed.
- Malicious entities violate the privacy of legitimate users and gain the ability to track their actual movements.
- Handheld devices, which are easily stolen, reveal sensitive information.

Copyright © 2004, Idea Group Inc. Copying or distributing in print or electronic forms without written permission of Idea Group Inc. is prohibited.

Integrity compromises occur if:

- Malicious entities gain unauthorized access to an organization's computer network through wireless connections, bypassing any firewall protections.
- Malicious entities steal the identity of legitimate users and masquerade on internal or external corporate networks.
- Sensitive data are corrupted during improper synchronization.
- Data are extracted without detection from improperly configured devices.
- Viruses or other malicious code corrupt data on a wireless device and are introduced to a wired network connection.

Availability is reduced if:

- Denials of service (DoS) attacks are directed at wireless connections or devices.
- Malicious entities, through wireless connections, connect to other organizations for the purposes of launching attacks and concealing their activity.
- Interlopers, from insider or out, are able to gain connectivity to network management controls and thereby disable or disrupt operations (NIST Special Publication 800-48).

As WLANs become widespread, the need of business for a more robust security solution is required. Recent demonstrations of the vulnerability of Wired Equivalent Privacy (WEP) encryption make it clear that WEP protection alone is inadequate. The security features in WEP do not offer a high level of assurance. Fluhrer, Mantin and Shamir (2001) describe a passive cipher-text only attack on the RC4 stream cipher used in WEP. The authors stated, "Note that we have not attempted to attack an actual WEP connection, and hence do not claim that WEP is actually vulnerable

Copyright © 2004, Idea Group Inc. Copying or distributing in print or electronic forms without written permission of Idea Group Inc. is prohibited.

to this attack." Later, Stubblefield, Ioannidis and Rubin (2001) successfully implemented an attack, proving the complete vulnerability of WEP.

There is no need to fret about the design flaws identified in WEP. As a security service, WEP does what it was designed to do. As the name states, you get a level of privacy and security equivalent to that of wired LAN users. There were no guarantees and at the time the standard was published there may not have been anyone demanding guaranteed security features. For the WLAN, IEEE defined WEP to perform the following three functions:

- *Authentication:* A primary goal of WEP was to provide a security service to verify the identity of communicating client stations. This provides access control to the network by denying access to client stations that cannot authenticate properly. This service addresses the question, "Are only authorized persons allowed to gain access to my network?"
- *Confidentiality:* Confidentiality, or privacy, was a second goal of WEP. It was developed to provide "privacy achieved by a wired network". The intent was to prevent information compromise from casual eavesdropping (passive attack). This service, in general, addresses the question, "Are only authorized persons allowed to view my data?"
- *Integrity:* Another goal of WEP was a security service developed to ensure that messages are not modified in transit between the wireless clients and the access point in an active attack. This service addresses the question, "Is the data coming into or exiting the network trustworthy—has it been tampered with?" (Karygiannis & Owens, 2002).

Most of the complaints with WLAN security can be attributed to flaws in the design of the technology or specification. Weaknesses in the design are difficult to fix once the product is purchased. All technologies are

Copyright © 2004, Idea Group Inc. Copying or distributing in print or electronic forms without written permission of Idea Group Inc. is prohibited.

susceptible to have a design flaw. To overcome the design weakness, WLAN managers should take extra care to properly configure, implement and managed the network. It is impossible to completely identify all possible vulnerabilities when a product is purchased and before it is added to the network. However, once purchased there is unlimited time to 'tweak' the configuration or implementation with strong management practices. The next section discusses the different types of countermeasures available to mitigate some of the known vulnerabilities.

The best countermeasures involve management, implementation and configuration (MIC) activities to mitigate vulnerabilities in the WLAN. Management countermeasures should be applied based on a well-crafted security policy. The policy should be based on management's vision and give a framework for managing the WLAN. Managers then execute the vision by the way they implement controls and configure settings on the network.

Management Countermeasures

Management countermeasures set the stage for all that happens on the WLAN. Based on policy, these countermeasures should work to:

- Identify who may use WLAN technology in a corporation and limit access by function, location, and workgroup or security clearance.
- Identify whether Internet access is required beyond the WLAN network. Some WLAN applications are for intranets only.
- Describe who can install access points and other wireless equipment. With the ease of installation and configurations, it is important to verify proper use of the technology.
- Provide limitations on the location of and physical security for access points to minimize the propagation (distance and availability) of the signal.

Copyright © 2004, Idea Group Inc. Copying or distributing in print or electronic forms without written permission of Idea Group Inc. is prohibited.

- Describe the type of information that may be sent over wireless links to reduce compromises of sensitive data.
- Describe conditions under which wireless devices are allowed.
- Define standard security settings for access points to reduce risks and establish uniform configurations standards.
- Describe limitations on how the wireless device may be used, such as location in and outside the building and near sensitive areas, to gain access to personal or sensitive data.
- Describe the hardware and software configuration of all wireless devices.
- Provide guidelines on reporting losses of wireless devices and security incidents
- Provide guidelines for the protection of wireless clients to minimize/reduce theft.
- Provide guidelines on the use of encryption and key management systems.
- Define the frequency and scope of security assessments to include access point discovery.

Implementation Countermeasures

Implementation countermeasures are the controls in the process. Controls in WLAN management allow or restrict an activity or event from occurring. Think of all wireless networking as unsecured and publicly available. If possible move the access point into a DMZ (a protected sub-network on the LAN) where sensitive data are not available to attackers. Implement firewall protection to protect you from attacks and log attack attempts.

- Only use WAPs and NICs that support at least 64-bit (preferably a 128 bit) WEP.

Copyright © 2004, Idea Group Inc. Copying or distributing in print or electronic forms without written permission of Idea Group Inc. is prohibited.

- Consider using third-party encryption tools and third-party authentication before you permit communication with your access point.
- Try to physically locate the WAP so that its signal will be harder for a network sniffer to locate. Pay close attention to the orientation of the antenna; avoid locating the WAP near windows, or in a room adjacent to a street or parking lot.
- Do a periodic assessment of wireless networks in and around your workplace/home using a sniffer or employing a consulting service. It is easy for an employee to buy an NIC and a WAP and install them on a workstation. Some operating systems automatically bridge a WAP with the wired network, providing network access (behind the firewall) and proprietary information to anyone with a wireless card. An assessment will determine if security measures are in place, or if there have been any changes to the configuration. An assessment will also show how far wireless signals will travel outside your building.
- Purchase wireless technology that has flash upgradeable firmware. New security enhancements such as Wi-Fi Protected Access (WPA) are being developed, and with an upgradeable product, the likelihood of being able to use this technology is greater. Consider using WPA as it becomes available. WPA will have many new wireless security features, including authentication, key management, Temporal Key Integrity Protocol (TKIP), integrity checking, replay protection, and Advanced Encryption Standard (AES) encryption support.
- Ensure that your computers are running at the most current software patch level. This makes it harder to attack your systems and information if hackers gain access to the wireless network.
- Use an antivirus application with the most current virus and worm signature updates. This will help to prevent an attacker who has gained access to your network from installing a Trojan to gain back-door access to your computer, and will protect your computer from other malicious code.

Copyright © 2004, Idea Group Inc. Copying or distributing in print or electronic forms without written permission of Idea Group Inc. is prohibited.

- Restrict physical access to the access point; keep it out of sight and in a locked area. By restricting access to the WAP you will help to ensure that unauthorized persons are not able to physically reset, control, or reconfigure the device.

Configuration Countermeasures

Configuration countermeasures are the easiest to understand. The countermeasures address the authentication, access control, integrity and confidentiality of the data and hardware on the network. Understanding how to configure the access point is critical to meet the vision stated in your organization's security policy. Proper configuration will mitigate many threats and go a great distance to limit unforeseen, unanticipated vulnerabilities. A proactive approach is the best way to describe configuration countermeasures. Since instruction manuals come with most technology today, it should be easy to locate the specific settings by reading the manuals. Specific areas of interest include:

(1) *Enable WEP (wireless encryption protocol).* WEP minimizes the risk of radio frequency interception by somebody nearby. WEP is specified for encryption and authentication between clients and APs according to the 802.11 standard. WEP security is based on an encryption algorithm called RC4. Some products allow you to separately set the authentication method to shared key or open system. Use the "shared key" method so that encryption is used to both authenticate your client and encrypt its data. Even though WEP has been broken, it is a cost effective (free), and valuable first layer of security. In my research over the past three years, more than 60% of all access points do not use WEP; while enabling the service may cause an attacker or curious user to move on to an easier target. The encryption algorithm is generated based on a key (a number se-

Copyright © 2004, Idea Group Inc. Copying or distributing in print or electronic forms without written permission of Idea Group Inc. is prohibited.

quence) entered and controlled by the user. All clients and APs are configured with the same key to encrypt and decrypt transmissions of data. WEP keys are 40 or 128 bits in length and can be configured in three possible modes: no encryption mode, 40- bit or 128-bit encryption.

(2) *Secure your access point with a password.* Your access point should require a password to access its administrative features: if it does not, replace it with one that does. Use strong passwords to protect against password cracking tools. Make sure the access point is not using the default password. Default passwords are well known and will be one of the first exploits tried by an educated attacker. Many wireless detection devices identify the manufacturer based on the media access control (MAC) address; this information makes it easier to guess what type of WAP is being used, even if the SSID has been changed. Change your password periodically.

(3) *Change the SSID to a truly unique name that does not identify the owner of the access point.* The SSID allows a WLAN to be segmented into multiple networks, each with a different identifier. Each of these networks is assigned a unique identifier, which is programmed into one or more APs. To access any of the networks, a client computer must be configured with the corresponding SSID identifier for that network. Thus, SSID acts as a simple password, providing a measure of security. A weakness is created when the SSID is widely known or shared, and it is easily obtained by freeware loaded onto a wireless network client.

(4) *Disable "broadcast SSID" if this feature is supported by the equipment vendor.* Most access points broadcast SSID by default. This will accept any SSID. By disabling broadcast SSID, the SSID configured in the client must match the SSID of the access point.

(5) *Turn off dynamic host configuration protocol (DHCP) and assign a static IP address to wireless devices.* This will keep your

Copyright © 2004, Idea Group Inc. Copying or distributing in print or electronic forms without written permission of Idea Group Inc. is prohibited.

WAP from issuing an IP address to any computer that tries to connect with it. Also consider changing the IP subnet to a non-default address. Many access points default to the 192.168.1.0 network, and use 192.168.1.1 as the default router. Changing these defaults provides additional layers of security.

(6) *Filter devices based on the MAC address.* Filtering increases security by configuring an access point with a list of MAC addresses associated with the client computers that are allowed access to the access point. If a client's MAC address is not on the list, the access point will deny access. This method provides good security but is only suited to small networks. The labor-intensive work of entering MAC addresses and maintaining up-to-date lists on all of the access point devices obviously limits the scalability of this approach. An access point can be set up to provide encryption-only protection in open-system mode, or to add authentication in shared-key mode. MAC address filtering is often used together with this encryption. WEP security is best suited for small networks, as there is no key management protocol. As a result, keys must be manually entered into every client. This can be a huge management task, especially as keys should be changed regularly to provide a higher level of security.

Lengthen the beacon interval of your access point. Beacon frames announce the existence of your wireless network to all. These beacons are transmitted from access points at regular intervals and allow a client station to identify and match configuration parameters in order to join a wireless network. The interval length may be set to its highest value, resulting in an approximate 67-second interval.

As a more secure model, some vendors have developed VPN solutions that create a secure tunnel for your wireless traffic. An evolution of wireless security products now includes the means to authenticate all

Copyright © 2004, Idea Group Inc. Copying or distributing in print or electronic forms without written permission of Idea Group Inc. is prohibited.

wireless users before they can gain access to network resources, encrypt data prior to them passing through the air using the advanced encryption standard and controlling user access to network segments through the use of policy servers.

What is Next?

Many people are working to improve the security of the WLAN. The greatest reason is to upgrade the security functionality. To a lesser degree, but equally important, these efforts also promote assurance to the users and managers of wireless devices. Here are three approaches that have promise for the future of 802.11 WLAN.

nDosa

The future of secure WLAN may rest with products like nDosa Access Point. nDosa Technologies introduced a secure wireless LAN technology based on its nESA (nDosa Enhanced Security Algorithm) that renders its signal invisible to would-be hackers and unauthorized observers, and hence, greatly reduces its vulnerability to hacking and intrusion. It should be noted, however, that although some determined hackers may still be able observe the RF signal and monitor LAN activity over the air, it would be extremely difficult for them to break into the system (Kim & Shin, 2003). Like other WLAN solutions, it is scalable, upgradeable, flexible and can be customized.

nDosa secure WLAN users can access not only nDosa secure WLANs but also the standard WLANs deployed widely in public places or in highly secure areas. When needs arise to enhance authentication or key management procedure, nDosa secure WLAN technology can be

Copyright © 2004, Idea Group Inc. Copying or distributing in print or electronic forms without written permission of Idea Group Inc. is prohibited.

applied without alteration. Encryption algorithms and security solutions, in general, need to be upgraded continually as they are at war against hackers. According to the literature, nESA is designed to make upgrades simple and easy.

The combination of the proposed wireless LAN scheme with nDosa's existing secure wireless LAN technology would render the system not only invisible even in the RF band, but also assures that the system will remain relatively impervious to break-ins even if the signal is detected. Implementation of both security measures would provide the wireless LAN with ironclad security that is necessary and appropriate for defense of government applications and data.

WPA

Wi-Fi Protected Access is a specification of standards-based, interoperable security enhancements that strongly increase the level of data protection and access control for existing and future wireless LAN systems. Designed to run on existing hardware as a software upgrade, Wi-Fi Protected Access is derived from and will be forward compatible with the upcoming IEEE 802.11i standard (*http://www.wi-fi.org/OpenSection/pdf/Wi-Fi_Protected_Access_Overview.pdf*). WPA is a proactive response by the industry to offer an immediate and strong security solution. An inexpensive software upgrade is now available to installation at the enterprise or SOHO WLANs. This solution is compatible across multiple vendors and is configurable with authentication servers or as a stand-alone. WPA is a subset of the 802.11i draft standard and will maintain forward compatibility.

Wi-Fi Protected Access was constructed to provide an improved data encryption, which was weak in WEP, and to provide user authentication, which was largely missing in WEP. The improvements are centered

Copyright © 2004, Idea Group Inc. Copying or distributing in print or electronic forms without written permission of Idea Group Inc. is prohibited.

Table 1. Comparison Chart

	WEP	WPA	802.11i	nDOSA
Cipher	RC4	RC4	CTR-CCMP	nESA
Key Size	40 bits	128 bits encryption 64 bits authentication	128 bits	128 ~ 256 bits
Key Life	24-bit IV	48-bit IV	48-bits IV	48-bits IV
Packet Key	Concatenated	Mixing Function	Not Needed	Mixing Function
Data Integrity	CRC-32	Michael	CCM	CRC-32
Header Integrity	None	Michael	CCM	nESA
Replay Attack	None	IV Sequence	IV Sequence	Encrypted IV
Key Management	None	EAP	EAP	EAP & any other methods
Header Encryption	None	None	None	nESA
Hidden Mode	None	None	None	Yes

on the use of enhanced data encryption through Temporal Key Integrity Protocol (TKIP). TKIP provides important data encryption enhancements including a per-packet key mixing function, a message integrity check (MIC) named *Michael,* an extended initialization vector (IV) with sequencing rules, and a re-keying mechanism. Through these enhancements, TKIP addresses all WEP's known vulnerabilities.

Using the Enterprise-level User Authentication via 802.1x and Extensible Authentication Protocol (EAP) WEP has almost no user authentication mechanism, Wi-Fi Protected Access implements 802.1x and the EAP strengthens user authentication. Together, these implementations provide a framework for strong user authentication. This framework utilizes a central authentication server, such as RADIUS, to authenticate each user on the network before they join it, and also employs "mutual authentication" so that the wireless user does not accidentally join a rogue network that might steal its network credentials.

Copyright © 2004, Idea Group Inc. Copying or distributing in print or electronic forms without written permission of Idea Group Inc. is prohibited.

Defensive Enterprise Solutions

Many companies have developed enterprise WLAN solutions that address many of the vulnerabilities associated with 802.11b. The features of the enterprise require layers of defense. WLAN managers should acquire a software suite that meets a basic security architecture standard. At a minimum the solution should include:

- Mutual authentication of users and network
- Access control to access points and to resources on the wired network
- Roll based access control
- Authorization of users and devices
- Message confidentiality
- Message authentication
- Dynamic key management
- Isolation of wireless traffic from wire LAN
- High level cryptographic protocol

The Wireless Wall by Cranite System, Inc. is an enterprise wide WLAN solution. WirelessWall (*http://www.cranite.com/pdf/whitepapers/wirelesswall-tech-op.pdf*) is a suite of software solutions that are based on an open architecture. This solution is for managing and securing wireless networks that enable maximum mobility for users. WirelessWall interoperates with existing policy, management, and security applications and provides broad-based support for a wide variety of wireless devices.

Follow-Up Procedures

Security assessments and audits should be a part of the organization's security policies, and are the best way to measure the success of a WLAN

Copyright © 2004, Idea Group Inc. Copying or distributing in print or electronic forms without written permission of Idea Group Inc. is prohibited.

security plan. Assessments baseline the current security posture by evaluating the configuration against recognized industry standards and best practices.

The assessment is an excellent management tool that identifies where security is adequate and inadequate. Assessment results are then used to allow management to prioritize resources and efforts for the future. Assessments are essential for checking the security posture of a WLAN and for determining corrective action to make sure it remains secure. Audits verify the controls of a WLAN are working as described by the documentation. Auditors examine documentation, interview users and research historical trends to determine what the security plans are supposed to do. If the written controls are the same in operations, the audit is favorable.

However, if there is a disconnect between the written and operational activities, the audit is not favorable. It is important for corporations to perform regular audits using wireless network analyzers and other tools. An analyzer, sometimes called a "sniffer", is an effective tool to conduct security auditing and troubleshoot wireless network issues (Karygiannis & Owens, 2002). Security administrators or security auditors can use network analyzers to determine if wireless products are transmitting correctly and on the correct channels. Administrators should periodically check within the office building space (and campus) for rogue access points and against other unauthorized access methods.

Federal, state and local agencies may also consider using an independent third party to conduct the security audits. Independent third-party security consultants are often more up-to-date on security vulnerabilities, better trained on security solutions, and equipped to assess the security of a wireless network. An independent third-party audit, which may include penetration testing, will help an agency ensure that its WLAN is compliant with established security procedures and policies and that the system is up-to-date with the latest software patches and upgrades.

Copyright © 2004, Idea Group Inc. Copying or distributing in print or electronic forms without written permission of Idea Group Inc. is prohibited.

Conclusions

Wireless devices, WLAN and vulnerabilities are here to stay. More and more new applications are introduced using this technology across horizontal market. The demand on the WLAN is going to grow in the upcoming years as we try to determine how to make all these new devices work seamlessly with the enterprise. The faster organizations are able to generalize the challenges associated with WLANs, the stronger their security will be. Some of the vulnerabilities and threats are universal because vendors accept the 802.11b standard without making changes to the security services. Historical, well-documented problems are rubberstamped from device to device — great for the consumer and the vendor, but an eye-opening problem for new WLAN owners.

Planning and Managing Data Obsolescence

Organizations that own or use large databases and data warehouses face a major expense in the next three to 10 years as historical transactional data grow stale and require retirement away from production systems. Given the speed of creation for new information — despite remarkable new storage technologies that seems to create endless amounts of capacity — at some point in time it makes sense to remove information that is five, 10 or 20 years old, as its value is low.

From a security perspective, information that is deleted or removed from a networked system reduces the possibility of unauthorized access from that one system, but it creates new opportunities for theft, loss and mischief in other ways. Creating a formal process with multiple points of confirmation of security including an audit trail are critical elements of ensuring information assurance.

Copyright © 2004, Idea Group Inc. Copying or distributing in print or electronic forms without written permission of Idea Group Inc. is prohibited.

For example, information held by a bank on accounts closed 10 years ago probably can be completely removed from a production system and stored off-site in a secure location. Should there ever be a need for it—perhaps in a tax investigation or lawsuit—it could probably be retrieved and restored. But perhaps not.

If the master index for the file is lost or corrupted, the bank may not know where to look for the file. Or, assuming the index is usable, the tape, CDROM, or disk containing the file may have been removed from the storage facility. Even worse, the file could have been copied by unauthorized users and then returned to the storage facility without notice. The risk of loss has only shifted from a production system to the archive system.

Also, what about different physical or file formats that occur as technological advances quickly occur? In 1980, a high-density tape stored 6250 bits per inch. Today's tape backup devices store 100 times that density, and in a few years will exceed 1,000 times. Can the data stored at 6250 be restored to a new format? Yes, but at significant expense to the organization requesting the conversion. Obsolete hardware is often exchanged for new systems that are incompatible with very old formats and media types. Having an outsource company convert a few tapes or files may be possible, but what if you had 50,000 tapes or CDROMs? What if you did not know which one had the exact data you were looking for? For a very large company with multiple terabytes of retired information, the cost could exceed many hundreds of thousands of dollars to continually update storage indexes, upgrade tapes, CDROMs, and USB memory devices to ensure compatibility with modern equipment and formats.

Here are several concepts to keep in mind concerning the security of obsolete information:

(1) Establish information usage "lifetimes" and periodically remove information not needed today

Copyright © 2004, Idea Group Inc. Copying or distributing in print or electronic forms without written permission of Idea Group Inc. is prohibited.

(2) Use a logical storage index system for all files so that the location of a file or group of files can be easily determined, even if the master index is lost or corrected
(3) Ensure that different staff members perform various parts of the duplication, indexing, storage and verification so that each is checking the other's work
(4) Perform verification audits on the obsolescence process by periodically checking the ability to restore retired data onto new equipment and formats
(5) Ensure the security of the off-site security locations — use at least two to ensure information survival probability — through third-party audits and confidence tests
(6) When upgrading computer hardware (tape and disk storage), try to obtain the maximum backward compatibility guarantees possible to reduce the cost and effort required to upgrade retired information assets

Planning and Managing Data Backup and Recovery Protocols

While simple in concept, saving and restoring large amounts of information (more than five gigabytes per day) requires significant process and repetition protocols to ensure systems can operate when unexpected events occur. Restores are needed when computer hardware suffers a serious mechanical or electrical failure, environmental accidents occur (such as fire sprinkler pipes breaking and flooding the computer room) or when malicious attacks are launched against the organization and its facilities.

Storing information from a production system used 24×7 must be scheduled with a plan that assumes some data cannot be saved due to the

Copyright © 2004, Idea Group Inc. Copying or distributing in print or electronic forms without written permission of Idea Group Inc. is prohibited.

locking nature of relational databases during transactions that prevent copying. Also, the process of backing up data may impact system performance, which may impact user productivity and customer satisfaction.

The complexity of the restore depends in large part on how much information is being restored: does one file, one disk drive, one system or everything need to be restored? Does the restore period cover one day, one week, or one month? Or more? Do backup tapes or CDROMs need to be brought to the computer room, or are they stored inside the room? Does anyone know where they are kept, and what files are stored on which storage devices?

Where this gets interesting to management is after funding large IT budgets for years, data cannot be restored due to equipment malfunctions, incomplete or missing backup files, or lack of process. From a security perspective, not being able to restore information when needed — no matter what the reason — places the organization at a high risk of business failure or financial impact.

What should be done to reduce the risk of data loss and business impact due to poor backup and restoration? Several paths can be followed:

(1) Use the 80-20 rule to determine what must be backed up daily (or hourly) and what can wait for a longer cycle
(2) Test tape and CDROM hardware weekly for defective operations or irregular reliability
(3) Test backup copies on different systems to ensure they can be read by any system — not just the one that wrote the files
(4) Clearly label each backup storage device along with an index of the file names and types on the device
(5) Keep all backup storage devices in a safe and secure location away from accidental damage, theft, or corruption
(6) Make multiple copies of the indexes and place them in different secured cabinets or locations

Copyright © 2004, Idea Group Inc. Copying or distributing in print or electronic forms without written permission of Idea Group Inc. is prohibited.

(7) Every six months have the equipment manufacturer verify their equipment is operational, storage devices are correctly used, and recovery processes are appropriate
(8) From a security perspective, ensure system operations will not be interrupted by the loss of data or processing capacity due to security breaches or attacks

Biometrics

Biometrics refers to the technologies that can identify and verify physical parts of the human body or their corresponding traits or behavior. These technologies include fingerprint readers, facial scanners, retina scanners, signature and voiceprint digitizers. They work by comparing a digital sample provided to them by the user and automatically verify it against a database of "known" identities. If there is a match, the user is recognized and "identified". If not, the system may save the digital information for further processing to determine who the user was.

Biometrics has been a technology on the verge of acceptance for several years, but high costs and questions about its reliability have constrained widespread commercial acceptance. During the past five years, these concerns have been addressed through technical improvements, with false positives (incorrectly identifying one person as another) and false rejections (incorrectly rejecting the correct person) now in the acceptable range of 99.9%, as needed for commercial application.

Biometric security is considered to be one of the most secure methods of identification, as it verifies something that you do, and something that you are. For example, your signature and your typing pattern is something you do. Your fingerprint, facial characteristics, voice and eye profile are things that you are. Biometric identifiers are far better at protecting access than passwords or physical devices such as badges or keys as they are far more

Copyright © 2004, Idea Group Inc. Copying or distributing in print or electronic forms without written permission of Idea Group Inc. is prohibited.

difficult to steal or share. When combined with other methods of identification, biometric techniques provide strong defense against unauthorized access to information, systems and networks.

Biometric measurements are usually classified into four domains:

(1) Universality: virtually all people should be able to use the system
(2) Uniqueness: no people should have the exact same characteristic
(3) Permanence: the characteristic should be resilient over time
(4) Collectability: the characteristic should be measurable quantitatively

When selecting which biometric factor to identify, system suppliers also look at device performance (speed, accuracy and reliability); acceptability of the device to users (is it invasive, dangerous, offensive); and circumvention (to what degree users can fool the system). Regardless of device type, the biometric identification process works the same way:

A sample is taken of the person's biometric characteristic, and transformed into a mathematical code that will be used as the "match". When the user wants to access the system, he or she provides a new sample — such as a fingerprint — which is compared against the sample. If it matches, access is granted to the user. If not, a challenge question or a second match may be requested to verify the user's identity. If the second match fails, access is denied.

Where should biometric technology be used? Although it can be deployed everywhere, the most cost effective places are where the user's identity must absolutely be verified. Examples include a pharmacist filling a prescription, a financial trader trusted to move millions of dollars in trades every day, people with a need-to-know security clearance, and convicted prisoners who might have a similar name or visual appearance as someone else to prevent them from leaving prison in their place.

Typical security applications in the IT world include access control to computer rooms and facilities, access to computer networks and systems,

Copyright © 2004, Idea Group Inc. Copying or distributing in print or electronic forms without written permission of Idea Group Inc. is prohibited.

and as a single sign-on method for users who use multiple systems with unique identification methods.

SmartCards

Known by different names, SmartCards are credit-card sized access devices that provide a portable, erasable memory device. Combined with a user provided password or biometric, the card can contain encryption algorithms, biometric templates, medical histories, purchase profiles, and other information that enhances the user's ability to access information in a secure and convenient way (rather than carrying a notebook computer around). SmartCards can be reprogrammed as they are used, so that every time it accesses a system it can be changed to a new encrypted code, substantially increasing the difficulty of reusing it.

Why these cards are important concerns the choices management has in upgrading system access from pure passwords to a combination of technology and user identification codes. SmartCards are relatively inexpensive (about $5.00 to $20.00 depending on type), convenient and durable. Moving from a password-only environment to a biometric enhanced system may involve an investment of $250 to $500 per workstation. Upgrading to a SmartCard environment is much cheaper, but of course does not provide the advantages that biometrics offer.

Security System Verification

Often referred to as "Penetration Testing" or "Probe and Response" verification, this activity is a critical part of ensuring all of the plans and procedures that should be in place are in place. Usually performed by an

Copyright © 2004, Idea Group Inc. Copying or distributing in print or electronic forms without written permission of Idea Group Inc. is prohibited.

independent consulting or security organization to avoid undue political and management influence, system security verification often occurs upon a milestone event such as major software deployment or operating system upgrade. In the case of highly trusted information systems (DoD Orange Book categories B1, B2 and A) verifications occur on a random, but continuous basis to verify currency of software patches, closure of unneeded firewall ports, and password obsolescence, among other details.

Internal IT security organizations should plan routine audits as well to ensure system operational activities have not accidentally caused access exposures or opportunities. Hackers and crackers base many of their attacks on "assumptions" made by security professionals that software patches have been installed, unused modems have been removed, and terminated employee passwords have been deleted.

Findings from verification audits are grouped into "high", "medium" and "low" categories based on criticality of resolution. High findings are responded to and resolved immediately, medium as soon as practical and low as part of ongoing security development or deployment activities.

IT executives and senior managers should become familiar with the findings from verification audits and ask for the details on what was done to respond to every security finding. Scheduling and chairing monthly security briefings is an excellent approach to take to understand what is happening (or not happening) and why. There is an obvious investment of money and management time in holding these meetings — which should result in high value security activities being completed or planned. Given the continuous nature of security attacks and ways to respond to and repel them, it would be rare to not have several "active" items to discuss at both the technical and management levels of the organization.

Copyright © 2004, Idea Group Inc. Copying or distributing in print or electronic forms without written permission of Idea Group Inc. is prohibited.

Best Practices Framework

Best Practice	Criticality	Frequency	Participants	Activity Results
Verify all systems have current software security patches installed and activated	High	As needed	Security, system admins	Updated software patches on all systems as soon as practical
Assess and verify that operating system and application security settings on all production systems can only be changed by system administrators	High	Monthly	Security, system admins	Access for changes restricted to admins only
Locate and confirm data obsolescence policy and verify it is being followed	High	Quarterly	Management, security	Data are being retired with adequate safeguards
Test all data backup and recovery systems and verify operational practices are working to restore data	High	Monthly	Security, system admins	Confirmed ability to save and recover data
Locate and confirm receipt of all software licenses to ensure accurate license fees are being paid	Medium	Quarterly	Management, finance, system admins	Compliance with software license terms and conditions
Locate and verify that processes to provide system access are reasonable and that undue security exposure has been avoided	Medium	Quarterly	Management, finance, system admins	Confidence that access is being provided to the correct people per policy
Verify that wireless access points have at least 64-bit encryption and have been located away from insecure areas	High	When installed; check quarterly	Security, system admins	Reduced exposure to wireless attack and unauthorized access
Disable "Broadcast SSID" features from wireless access points	High	When installed; check quarterly	Security, system admins	Reduced exposure to wireless attack and unauthorized access
Determine if implementing a biometric or SmartCard access method is appropriate, based on the value of information and number of users/customers that could be impacted	Medium	Quarterly	Management, finance, system admins	Determine if security methods should be upgraded due to changing business conditions

Copyright © 2004, Idea Group Inc. Copying or distributing in print or electronic forms without written permission of Idea Group Inc. is prohibited.

Summary

The technology aspects of information security continue to increase in complexity, performance, and capability, matching the requirements of the market. While amazing what they can do on a 24x7 basis to stop authorized access, monitor intrusive activities for evidence and prosecution, and transmit gigabytes of data almost instantly, these system are just electronic devices. They require substantial engineering support and maintenance, upgrades and above all, management direction.

The raging battle between groups and individuals trying to gain access to information assets and systems they should not have access to and organizations working very hard to keep them out is almost unknown to senior executives and managers who have many other responsibilities to manage. Small companies in the United States report 200 to 500 hits against their firewalls each hour by unidentified intrusion search engines seeking to find cracks in their firewall that can be leveraged into full access. It is hard to fathom the hundreds of thousands of intrusive searches hits per day that large financial and government organizations successfully stave off with little public mention or attention.

It is also clear that a combination of technology harnessed to basic common sense and attention to detail goes a long way towards closing most of the largest security holes in the information infrastructure. Holes remain, but making the reward smaller than the effort required to obtain it usually stops hackers from wasting their time to gain little.

In the coming years, senior executives and managers will need to become familiar with the overall concepts and terminology of information security to better understand why they should support increased investments in equipment and staffing. According to experts in law, technology and business, computer security will remain a critical component of every IT organization for decades to come.

Copyright © 2004, Idea Group Inc. Copying or distributing in print or electronic forms without written permission of Idea Group Inc. is prohibited.

Chapter VII

Reference Materials

FBI Statement on Improving Information Security

(Farnan, 2003)

*April 3, 2003. Statement for the Record of James E. Farnan, Deputy Assistant Director, Cyber Division, Federal Bureau of Investigation on **Fighting Fraud: Improving Information Security.** Before the House Financial Services Committee, Subcommittee on Financial Institutions and Consumer Credit, and Oversight and Investigations, Washington, D.C.*

Thank you for inviting me here today to testify on the topic, "Fighting Fraud: Improving Information Security." Holding this hearing demonstrates your commitment to improving the security of our Nation's information systems and this committee's leadership on this issue in Congress. Our work here is vitally important because the stakes involved are enormous. My testimony today will address the activities of the FBI's Cyber Division

Copyright © 2004, Idea Group Inc. Copying or distributing in print or electronic forms without written permission of Idea Group Inc. is prohibited.

as they relate to a broad spectrum of criminal acts involving fraud and information security. Today there are over 180 million computer users in the United States alone. There are more than 600 million worldwide, and the number is growing. Many of these users are connecting to the Internet, communicating, conducting business, managing financial affairs, searching for information and, unfortunately, committing crimes.

Cyber Vulnerabilities

Anyone with a basic computer interest is probably aware of the existence of security vulnerabilities, at least in a general sense, in our networks and computers. These vulnerabilities are widely discussed in the media. Using a simple Internet search, a 12 year old could locate a variety of hacker tools, then download and implement them. When we first saw the dramatic increase in home computers in early 1990s, we did not worry about attacks on our family computers. Most casual users were not aware that security vulnerabilities even existed. Today, we worry about our systems getting hit with viruses, worms and Trojans. Companies secure web sites and web pages against attacks and defacements. Consumers are concerned that companies are not maintaining adequate security on our personal and financial information as we hear weekly news reports about hackers and new intrusions.

American consumers and businesses increasingly are relying on the Internet to complete transactions. E-commerce is growing in all sectors of the U.S. economy. Most e-commerce transactions are business-to-business (B2B), but e-commerce retail sales reached $46 billion in 2002, up from $36 billion in 2001. When Internet users — be they businesses or consumers — are crippled by Internet fraud schemes, the viability of e-commerce is compromised.

Computer intrusions are a different category from most fraud schemes. Many intrusions are never reported because companies fear a loss of

Copyright © 2004, Idea Group Inc. Copying or distributing in print or electronic forms without written permission of Idea Group Inc. is prohibited.

business from reduced consumer confidence in their security measures or from a fear of lawsuits. Most of the outsider-intrusions cases opened today are the result of a failure to patch a known vulnerability for which a patch has been issued. Theft of consumer information from a computer system can only be facilitated two ways: by insiders or by outside hackers. Insiders have various motivations, including retribution and money. Outsiders are usually motivated by challenge and/or greed.

The National Research Council issued a report in 2001 titled, "Cybersecurity Today and Tomorrow: Pay Now or Pay Later." If you have not seen the report, I would urge you to obtain a copy. The report makes a number of significant points and general observations, including a key one for this Hearing:

"Note also that an attacker ... may be able to exploit a flaw accidentally introduced into a system. System design and/or implementation that is poor by accident can result in serious security problems that can be deliberately target[ed] in a penetration attempt by an attacker."

If security on a system is inadequate, and someone chooses to exploit the weaknesses, consequences are inevitable. According to the report, there are three things that can go wrong with a computer system or network:

1. It can become unavailable or very slow. That is, using the system or network at all becomes impossible, or nearly so.
2. It can become corrupted, so that it does the wrong thing or gives wrong answers. For example, data stored on the computer may become different from what it should be, as would be the case if medical or financial records were improperly modified.
3. It can become leaky. That is, someone who should not have access to some or all of the information available through the network obtains such access.

Copyright © 2004, Idea Group Inc. Copying or distributing in print or electronic forms without written permission of Idea Group Inc. is prohibited.

When one of these things happen, the FBI is in a unique position to respond because it is the only Federal agency that has the statutory authority, expertise, and ability to combine the counterterrorism, counterintelligence, and criminal resources needed to effectively neutralize, mitigate, and disrupt illegal computer-supported operations.

The FBI's Cyber Division

The FBI's reorganization of the last two years included the goal of making our cyber investigative resources more effective. In 2002, the reorganization resulted in the creation of the FBI's Cyber Division.

The Cyber Division addresses cyber threats in a coordinated manner, allowing the FBI to stay technologically one step ahead of the cyber adversaries threatening the United States. The Cyber Division addresses all violations with a cyber nexus, which often have international facets and national economic implications. The Cyber Division also simultaneously supports FBI priorities across program lines, assisting counterterrorism, counterintelligence, and other criminal investigations when aggressive technological investigative assistance is required. The Cyber Division will ensure that agents with specialized technology skills are focused on cyber related matters.

At the Cyber Division we are taking a two-tracked approach to the problem. One avenue is identified as traditional criminal activity that has migrated to the Internet, such as Internet fraud, on-line identity theft, Internet child pornography, theft of trade secrets, and other similar crimes. The other, non-traditional approach consists of Internet-facilitated activity that did not exist prior to the establishment of computers, networks, and the World Wide Web. This encompasses "cyber terrorism," terrorist threats, foreign intelligence operations, and criminal activity precipitated by illegal computer intrusions into U.S. computer networks, including the disruption of computer supported operations and the theft of sensitive data via the

Copyright © 2004, Idea Group Inc. Copying or distributing in print or electronic forms without written permission of Idea Group Inc. is prohibited.

Internet. The FBI assesses the cyber-threat to the U.S. to be rapidly expanding, as the number of actors with the ability to utilize computers for illegal, harmful, and possibly devastating purposes is on the rise.

To accomplish its mission, the Cyber Division will form and maintain public/private alliances in conjunction with enhanced education and training to maximize counterterrorism, counterintelligence, and law enforcement cyber response capabilities. The FBI will also maximize the success of cyber investigations through awareness and exploitation of emerging technology.

To support this mission we are dramatically increasing our cyber training program and international investigative efforts. Consequently, specialized units are now being created at FBI Headquarters to provide training not only to FBI cyber squads, but also to the other agencies participating in existing or new cyber-related task forces in which the FBI is a participant. This training will largely be provided to investigators in the field. A number of courses will be provided at the FBI Academy at Quantico.

A typical case will come to the FBI through the Internet Fraud Complaint Center (IFCC), In its fourth year of operation, IFCC has proven to be a very successful clearinghouse, receiving over 75,000 complaints in 2002 on crimes ranging from identity theft and computer intrusions to child pornography.

If the IFCC received an intrusion report from a company in Birmingham, Alabama, we would first attempt to locate where the intrusion took place. That same company may have its servers in Minneapolis, while the intruder is routing attacks through Internet providers in California and Europe. If the servers in Minneapolis were hacked, the Minneapolis Cyber Crime Task Force would be assigned the lead on the case. The leads could start in California, but end up in Eastern Europe, Nigeria or even back to Birmingham, if an insider was involved. One of the FBI's Computer Analysis Response Teams (CART) would be called upon to preserve

Copyright © 2004, Idea Group Inc. Copying or distributing in print or electronic forms without written permission of Idea Group Inc. is prohibited.

computer forensic evidence, and that evidence could be forwarded to one of our new Regional Crime Forensic Labs, now located in Chicago, Dallas and San Diego. The Lab would determine the extent and duration of the intrusion, and whether the attacker came from inside or outside the company. Depending on the sophistication of the intruder, the case can be cracked in a few days or take years. Cases are routinely complex, and often involve international connections. The following cases serve as examples of typical cyber crimes:

Raymond Torricelli, aka "rolex"

Raymond Torricelli, aka "rolex," the head of a hacker group known as "#conflict," was convicted for, among other things, breaking into two computers owned and maintained by the National Aeronautics and Space Administration's Jet Propulsion Laboratory ("JPL"), located in Pasadena, California, and using one of those computers to host an Internet chat-room devoted to hacking.

Torricelli admitted that, in 1998, he was a computer hacker, and a member of a hacking organization known as "#conflict." Torricelli admitted that he used his personal computer to run programs designed to search the Internet, and seek out computers which were vulnerable to intrusion. Once such computers were located, Torricelli's computer obtained unauthorized access to the computers by uploading a program known as "rootkit." The file, "rootkit," is a program which, when run on computer, allows a hacker to gain complete access to all of a computer's functions without having been granted these privileges by the authorized users of that computer.

One of the computers Torricelli accessed was used by NASA to perform satellite design and mission analysis concerning future space missions, another was used by JPL's Communications Ground Systems Section as an e-mail and internal web server. After gaining this unauthorized access to computers and loading "rootkit," Torricelli, under his alias "rolex," used many of the computers to host chat-room discussions.

Copyright © 2004, Idea Group Inc. Copying or distributing in print or electronic forms without written permission of Idea Group Inc. is prohibited.

Torricelli admitted that, in these discussions, he invited other chat participants to visit a web site which enabled them to view pornographic images and that he earned 18 cents for each visit a person made to that web site. Torricelli earned approximately $300-400 per week from this activity. Torricelli also pled guilty to intercepting usernames and passwords traversing the computer networks of a computer owned by San Jose State University. In addition, Torricelli pled guilty to possession of stolen passwords and usernames which he used to gain free Internet access, or to gain unauthorized access to still more computers.

Torricelli admitted that when he obtained passwords which were encrypted, he would use a password cracking program known as "John-the-Ripper" to decrypt the passwords. He also pled guilty to possessing stolen credit card numbers that he obtained from other individuals and stored on his computer. Torricelli admitted that he used one such credit card number to purchase long distance telephone service.

Much of the evidence obtained against Torricelli was obtained through a search of his personal computer. In addition to thousands of stolen passwords and numerous credit card numbers, investigators found transcripts of chat-room discussions in which Torricelli and members of "#conflict" discussed, among other things, (1) breaking into other computers; (2) obtaining credit card numbers belonging to other persons and using those numbers to make unauthorized purchases; and (3) using their computers to electronically alter the results of the annual MTV Movie Awards. This case illustrates the wide variety of criminal acts which can result from security vulnerabilities.

Raphael Gray, aka "Curador"

On March 1, 2000, a computer hacker using the name "Curador" compromised several e-commerce web sites in the U.S., Canada, Thailand, Japan and the United Kingdom, and stole as many as 28,000 credit card numbers with losses estimated to be at least $3.5 million. Thousands

Copyright © 2004, Idea Group Inc. Copying or distributing in print or electronic forms without written permission of Idea Group Inc. is prohibited.

of credit card numbers and expiration dates were posted to various Internet web sites. After an extensive investigation, on March 23, 2000, the FBI assisted the Dyfed Powys (Wales, UK) Police Service in a search at the residence of "Curador," Raphael Gray. Mr. Gray, age 18, was arrested and charged in the UK along with a coconspirator under the UK's Computer Misuse Act of 1990. This case illustrates the benefits of law enforcement and private industry around the world working together in partnership on computer crime investigations.

Bloomberg Extortion

Kazakhstan citizens Oleg Zezov, and Igor Yarimaka were arrested on August 10, 2000 in London, England for breaking into Bloomberg L.P.'s Manhattan computer system in an attempt to extort money from Bloomberg. Zezov gained unauthorized access to the internal Bloomberg Computer System from computers located in Almaty, Kazakhstan. In the Spring of 1999, Bloomberg provided database services, via a system known as the "Open Bloomberg," to Kazkommerts Securities located in Almaty, Kazakhstan. Zezov was employed by Kazkommerts.

Zezov sent a number of e-mails to Michael Bloomberg, the founder and owner of Bloomberg, using the name "Alex," demanding that Bloomberg pay him $200,000 in exchange for providing information to Bloomberg concerning how Zezov was able to infiltrate Bloomberg's computer system. Michael Bloomberg sent e-mail to Zezov suggesting that they meet. Zezov demanded that Michael Bloomberg deposit $200,000 into an offshore account. Bloomberg established an account at Deutsche Bank in London and deposited $200,000. Michael Bloomberg suggested that they resolve the matter in London and Zezov agreed.

On August 6, 2000, Yarimaka and Zezov flew from Kazakhstan to London. On August 10, 2000, Yarimaka and Zezov met with officials from Bloomberg L.P., including Michael Bloomberg, and two London Metropolitan police officers, one posing as a Bloomberg L.P. executive and the

Copyright © 2004, Idea Group Inc. Copying or distributing in print or electronic forms without written permission of Idea Group Inc. is prohibited.

other serving as a translator. At the meeting, Yarimaka allegedly claimed that he was a former Kazakhstan prosecutor and explained that he represented "Alex" and would handle the terms of payment. According to the Complaint, Yarimaka and Zezov reiterated their demands at the meeting. Shortly after the meeting Yarimaka and Zezov were arrested. On February 27, 2003, the trial of Anatoljevich Zezev concluded with a guilty verdict for computer fraud, extortion, use of interstate communications for extortion, and conspiracy. He faces a maximum of 28 years in prison. This case is an example of a traditional crime facilitated by a computer.

Cyber crime continues to grow at an alarming rate, and security vulnerabilities contribute to the problem. We encourage administrators and security professionals to reduce opportunities for criminals by employing best practices and patching vulnerabilities before they can be exploited. The FBI will continue to aggressively pursue cyber criminals as we strive to stay one step ahead of them in the cyber crime technology race.

I thank you for your invitation to speak to you today and on behalf of the FBI look forward to working with you on this very important topic.

Computer Crime Statistics

An excellent reference source for computer crimes statistics is the Computer Security Institute web site, located at *www.gocsi.com*. The site has links to their annual computer crime survey that they conduct with the FBI's National Infrastructure Protection Center (NICP). The NICP is a partnership between industry and multiple federal agencies and intended to be a primary organization for responding to computerized crimes and attacks targeted against the nation's operational infrastructure, including airports, highways, telecommunications networks and government buildings.

Copyright © 2004, Idea Group Inc. Copying or distributing in print or electronic forms without written permission of Idea Group Inc. is prohibited.

The annual survey, downloadable for free from CSI, provides illuminating information on — among other findings — the types of computer crimes committed, possible sources, when they and who they are reported to, and the value of the loss. The survey is conducted every year and published in late March, early April. When published, the report has often become a media source for predicting computer crime trends and prevention techniques, measuring increases in crime occurence from year-to-year, and projecting financial losses should security countermeasures not succeed.

Firewall Reference Sources

There are several books that provide excellent general knowledge about firewalls. They include:

Cheswick, B., & Bellovin, S. (1994). *Firewalls and Internet security: Repelling the wily hacker.* ISBN 0-201-63357-4. Addison Wesley.

Garfinkel, S., & Spafford, G. (1996). *Practical Internet & Unix security.* ISBN 1-56592-148-8. O'Reilly Books.

Zwicky, E.D., Cooper, S., & Chapman, D.B. (2000). *Building Internet firewalls* (2nd ed.). ISBN1-56592-871-7. O'Reilly Books.

Additional related references are:

Comer, D., & Stevens, D. (1992). *Internetworking with TCP/IP* (vols. I, II, III). ISBN 0-13-468505-9 (I), 0-13-472242-6 (II), 0-13-474222-2 (III). Prentice-Hall. (A detailed discussion on the architecture and implementation of the Internet and its protocols. Volume I on principles, protocols and architecture is readable by everyone. Volume 2 (on design, implementation and internals) is more technical. Volume 3 covers client-server computing.)

Curry, D. (1992). *Unix system security — A guide for users and system administrators.* ISBN 0-201-56327-4. Addison Wesley.

Copyright © 2004, Idea Group Inc. Copying or distributing in print or electronic forms without written permission of Idea Group Inc. is prohibited.

Information on Firewalls from the Internet

Firewalls Mailing List (Curtin, 2000) *http://lists.gnac.net/firewalls.* The Internet firewalls mailing list is a forum for firewall administrators and implementers. To subscribe to Firewalls, send "subscribe firewalls" in the body of a message (not in the Subject line) to *majordomo@lists.gnac.net*

Firewall "How-to" Information

*http://sunsite.unc.edu/LDP/HOWTO/Firewall-HOWTO.html.*_Describes exactly what is needed to build a firewall, particularly using Linux. Firewall Toolkit (FWTK) and Firewall Papers: ftp://ftp.tis.com/pub/firewalls/

Marcus Ranum's firewall related publications: *http://www.ranum.com/pubs/*

Papers on Firewalls and Break-Ins

ftp://ftp.research.att.com/dist/internet_security/

Texas A&M University security tools: *http://www.net.tamu.edu/ftp/security/TAMU/*

COAST Project Internet Firewalls page: http://www.cs.purdue.edu/coast/firewalls/

Glossary of Security Terms

[Some of these terms were retrieved from SetSolutions, Inc. (2004)]

Abuse of Privilege. When a user performs an action that they should not have, according to organizational policy or law.

Access Control Lists. Rules for packet filters (typically routers) that define which packets to pass and which to block.

Copyright © 2004, Idea Group Inc. Copying or distributing in print or electronic forms without written permission of Idea Group Inc. is prohibited.

Access Router. A router that connects your network to the external Internet.

Application-Layer Firewall. A firewall system in which service is provided by processes that maintain complete TCP connection state and sequencing. Application layer firewalls often readdress traffic so that outgoing traffic appears to have originated from the firewall, rather than the internal host.

Authentication. The process of determining the identity of a user that is attempting to access a system.

Authentication Token. A portable device used for authenticating a user. Authentication tokens operate by challenge/response, time-based code sequences, or other techniques. This may include paper-based lists of onetime passwords.

Authorization. The processes of determining what types of activities are permitted. Usually, authorization is in the context of authentication: once you have authenticated a user, they may be authorized different types of access or activity.

Bastion Host. A system that has been hardened to resist attack, and which is installed on a network in such a way that it is expected to potentially come under attack. Bastion hosts are often components of firewalls, or may be outside Web servers or public access systems. Generally, a bastion host is running some form of general purpose operating system (e.g., Unix, VMS, NT, etc.) rather than a ROM-based or firmware operating system.

Challenge/Response. An authentication technique whereby a server sends an unpredictable challenge to the user, who computes a response using some form of authentication token.

Cryptographic Checksum. A one-way function applied to a file to produce a unique "fingerprint" of the file for later reference. Checksum systems are a primary means of detecting filesystem tampering on Unix.

Copyright © 2004, Idea Group Inc. Copying or distributing in print or electronic forms without written permission of Idea Group Inc. is prohibited.

Data Driven Attack. A form of attack in which the attack is encoded in innocuous-seeming data, which is executed by a user or other software to implement an attack. In the case of firewalls, a data driven attack is a concern since it may get through the firewall in data form and launch an attack against a system behind the firewall.

Defense in Depth. The security approach whereby each system on the network is secured to the greatest possible degree. May be used in conjunction with firewalls.

DNS Spoofing. Assuming the DNS name of another system by either corrupting the name service cache of a victim system, or by compromising a domain name server for a valid domain.

Encrypting Router. See Tunneling Router and Virtual Network Perimeter.

Firewall. A system or combination of systems that enforces a boundary between two or more networks.

Host-based Security. The technique of securing an individual system from attack. Host-based security is operating system and version dependent.

Insider Attack. An attack originating from inside a protected network.

Intrusion Detection. Detection of break-ins or break-in attempts either manually or via software expert systems that operate on logs or other information available on the network.

IP Splicing/Hijacking. An attack in which an active, established session is intercepted and co-opted by the attacker. IP splicing attacks may occur after an authentication has been made, permitting the attacker to assume the role of an already authorized user. Primary protections against IP splicing rely on encryption at the session or network layer.

IP Spoofing. An attack whereby a system attempts to illicitly impersonate another system by using its IP network address.

Least Privilege. Designing operational aspects of a system to operate with a minimum amount of system privilege. This reduces the authorization

Copyright © 2004, Idea Group Inc. Copying or distributing in print or electronic forms without written permission of Idea Group Inc. is prohibited.

level at which various actions are performed and decreases the chance that a process or user with high privileges may be caused to perform unauthorized activity resulting in a security breach.

Logging. The process of storing information about events that occurred on the firewall or network.

Log Processing. How audit logs are processed, searched for key events, or summarized.

Log Retention. How long audit logs are retained and maintained.

Network-Layer Firewall. A firewall in which traffic is examined at the network protocol packet layer.

Perimeter-based Security. The technique of securing a network by controlling access to all entry and exit points of the network.

Policy. Organization-level rules governing acceptable use of computing resources, security practices, and operational procedures.

Proxy. A software agent that acts on behalf of a user. Typical proxies accept a connection from a user, make a decision as to whether or not the user or client IP address is permitted to use the proxy, perhaps does additional authentication, and then completes a connection on behalf of the user to a remote destination.

Session Stealing. See IP Splicing. Social Engineering. An attack based on deceiving users or administrators at the target site. Social engineering attacks are typically carried out by telephoning users or operators and pretending to be an authorized user, to attempt to gain illicit access to systems.

Steganography. Computer steganography is based on two principles. The first one is that the files that contain digitized images or sound can be altered to a certain extent without losing their functionality, unlike other types of data that have to be exact in order to function properly. The other principle deals with the human inability to distinguish minor changes in image color or sound quality.

Copyright © 2004, Idea Group Inc. Copying or distributing in print or electronic forms without written permission of Idea Group Inc. is prohibited.

Trojan Horse. A software entity that appears to do something normal but which, in fact, contains a trapdoor or attack program.

Tunneling Router. A router or system capable of routing traffic by encrypting it and encapsulating it for transmission across an untrusted network, for eventual de-encapsulation and decryption.

Virtual Network Perimeter. A network that appears to be a single protected network behind firewalls, which actually encompasses encrypted virtual links over untrusted networks.

Virus. A replicating code segment that attaches itself to a program or data file. Viruses might or might not contain attack programs or trapdoors.

Worm. A stand-alone program that, when run, copies itself from one host to another, and then runs itself on each newly infected host. The widely reported "Internet Virus" of 1988 was not a virus at all, but actually a worm.

Frequently Asked Questions about Computer Viruses

The following list of FAQs is hosted at: *http://www.faqs.org/*

Computer Virus FAQ for New Users

http://www.faqs.org/faqs/computer-virus/new-users/

Virus-L/comp.virus FAQ v2.00

http://www.faqs.org/faqs/computer-virus/faq/

Viruses and the Mac FAQ

http://www.faqs.org/faqs/computer-virus/macintosh-faq/

alt.comp.virus Mini-FAQ

http://www.faqs.org/faqs/computer-virus/mini-faq/

alt.comp.virus FAQ Part 1/4

http://www.faqs.org/faqs/computer-virus/alt-faq/part1/

alt.comp.virus FAQ Part 2/4

http://www.faqs.org/faqs/computer-virus/alt-faq/part2/

Copyright © 2004, Idea Group Inc. Copying or distributing in print or electronic forms without written permission of Idea Group Inc. is prohibited.

alt.comp.virus FAQ Part 3/4

http://www.faqs.org/faqs/computer-virus/alt-faq/part3/

alt.comp.virus FAQ Part 4/4

http://www.faqs.org/faqs/computer-virus/alt-faq/part4/

Hoax and Chain Letter Databases

The US CERT Coordination Center receives many calls and e-mails from people asking whether or not a message they received via e-mail is true or not. The following list of resources can help you separate the hoaxes from the valid warnings.

Charles Hymes' Hoaxes
http://www.nonprofit.net/hoax
CIAC (Computer Incident Advisory Capability)
Internet Hoaxes — how to identify a new hoax or valid warning and what to do
http://hoaxbusters.ciac.org/HBHoaxInfo.html
IBM antivirus online — hype alerts!
http://www.av.ibm.com/BreakingNews/HypeAlert/
ICSA - Hoax Information
http://www.icsa.net/html/communities/antivirus/hoaxes/
Internet Chain Letters — how to recognize a new chain letter, what to do
http://hoaxbusters.ciac.org/HBHoaxInfo.html
McAfee - Virus Information Library - Virus Hoaxes
http://vil.mcafee.com/hoax.asp
Network Associates - Virus Library - Hoaxes
http://www.nai.com/asp_set/anti_virus/library/hoaxes.asp

Virus Organizations and Publications

EICAR (European Institute for Computer Anti-Virus Research)
http://www.eicar.com/

Copyright © 2004, Idea Group Inc. Copying or distributing in print or electronic forms without written permission of Idea Group Inc. is prohibited.

EICAR combines universities, industry and media plus technical, security and legal experts from civil and military government and law enforcement as well as privacy protection organizations whose objectives are to unite non-commercial efforts against writing and proliferation of malicious code like computer viruses or Trojan Horses, and against computer crime, fraud and the misuse of computers or networks, including malicious exploitation of personnel data, based on a code of conduct.

ICSA (International Computer Security Association)

http://www.icsa.net

http://www.icsa.net/html/communities/antivirus/

http://www.virusbtn.com/

The international publication on computer virus prevention, recognition and removal. *Virus Bulletin* is the technical journal on developments in the field of computer viruses and antivirus products

The WildList Organization International

http://www.wildlist.org/

The mission of the Wildlist Organization is to provide accurate, timely and comprehensive information about "In the Wild" computer viruses to both users and product developers. The WildList, a list of computer viruses found in the wild and reported by a diverse group of over 40 qualified volunteers, is made available free of charge by the organization.

Government Standards

NIST. *www.NIST.gov.* Common Criteria for Information Technology Security Evaluations, Standard 15408, Common Criteria, *http://csrc.ncsl.nist.gov / cc / ccv20 / cc2list.htm*

NIST. (1995). In B. Guttman & E. Roback, *An introduction to computer security: The NIST handbook.* SPEC PUB 800-12.

Copyright © 2004, Idea Group Inc. Copying or distributing in print or electronic forms without written permission of Idea Group Inc. is prohibited.

DoD Orange Book. DoD Trusted Computer System Evaluation Criteria, US Department of Defense DoD 5200.28-STD, published December 1985.

Organization for Economic Cooperation and Development (OECD, 1992). Guidelines for the security of information systems, OECD, OECD/GD (92) 190, Paris.

Red Book (1987). National Computer Security Center. Trusted Network Interpretation, NCSC, NCSC-TG-005, Version 1.0.

Incident Response Centers

CERT (sm) Coordination Center
http://www.cert.org/
e-mail: cert@cert.org
Phone: 412/268-7090

Computer Incident Advisory Capability (CIAC)
http://ciac.llni.gov/
e-mail: ciac@llnl.gov
Phone: 925/422-8193

Defense Information Systems Agency for Automated Systems Security Incident Support Team (ASSIST, for DoD sites)
http://www.assist.mil/
e-mail: cert@cert.mil
Phone: 800/357-4231

Department of Homeland Security
http://www.uscert.gov
e-mail: uscert@uscert.gov

Copyright © 2004, Idea Group Inc. Copying or distributing in print or electronic forms without written permission of Idea Group Inc. is prohibited.

Federal Computer Incident Response Capability (FedCIRC)
http://www.fedcirc.gov/
e-mail: fedcirc@fedcirc.gov
Phone: 888/282-0870

Forum of Incident Response and Security Teams (FIRST)
http://www.first.org
e-mail: first-sec@first.org

NASA Incident Response Center (NASIRC)
http://www-nasirc.nasa.gov/nasa/index.htm
e-mail: nasirc@nasirc.nasa.gov
Phone: 800/762-7472

Federal Bureau of Investigation (FBI) – National Infrastructure Protection Center (NIPC)
http://www.fbi.gov/nipe/index.htm
e-mail: nipc@fbi.gov

IT Security Professional Associations

ISSA: (*www.issa.org*)
SANS Institute: (*ww.sans.org*)
ICSA (International Computer Security Association): *http://www.icsa.net*
CSI (Computer Security Institute). (*www.gocsi.org*)

Copyright © 2004, Idea Group Inc. Copying or distributing in print or electronic forms without written permission of Idea Group Inc. is prohibited.

Useful Security Web Sites

http://www.infosyssec.org/infosysec/index.htm

http://www.certicom.com

http://www.counterpane.com

http://www.cs.purdue.edu/coast/

http://www.cs.georgetown.edu/~denning/crypto/index.html

http://www.ntbugtraq.com/

http://www.nsi.org/compsec.html

http://www.sans.org

http://www.securityportal.com

http://www.icsa.net/

http://www.itpolicy.gsa.gov

http://www.cit.nih.gov/security.html

http://cs-www.nist.gov/

http://www.bs.org/

http://www.RSA.com

http://www.telstra.com.au/info/security.html

References

Alliance, W.F. (2003). *Wi-Fi protected access: An overview*. Retrieved February 5, 2004, from *http://www.wi-fi.org/OpenSection/pdf/Wi-Fi_Protected_Access_Overview.pdf*

Al-Saleh, A. (2002). *Secure, seamless roaming leads to an ideal wireless experience*. Retrieved February 3, 2004, from *http://www.tmcnet.com/bizwatch/articles/090402a.htm*

Austin, R. (2001). *The iPremier company (a): Denial of service attack.* Harvard Business School, 9-601-114 (rev. June 13, 2002). Boston, MA: Harvard Business School Publishing.

Copyright © 2004, Idea Group Inc. Copying or distributing in print or electronic forms without written permission of Idea Group Inc. is prohibited.

Beach, G. (2003, April 1). Certify security. *CIO Magazine, 12,* 16.

Cranite. (2003). *WirelessWall® technical operation white paper.* Retrieved February 7, 2004, from *http://www.cranite.com/pdf/whitepapers/wirelesswall-tech-op.pdf*

Curtin, M., & Ranum, M.J. *Internet firewalls: Frequently asked questions.* Date: 2000/12/01 19:48:21. Revision: 10.0. Downloaded February 14, 2004 from *http://www.faqs.org/faqs/firewalls-faq/*

Farnan, J.E. *Fighting fraud: Improving information security*

Federal Bureau of Investigation, Washington, D.C. April 3, 2003. Downloaded on February 15, 2004 from *http://www.fbi.gov/congress/congress03/farnan040303.htm*

Fluhrer, S., Mantin, I., & Shamir, A. (2001). Weaknesses in the key scheduling algorithm of RC4. *Eighth Annual Workshop on Selected Areas in Cryptography.*

FTC. (2004). *Report on consumer complaints.*

Gehrke, R. (2003, November 6). Quick consumer notification key in identity theft cases, *USA Today.* Retrieved February 15, 2004 from *http://www.usatoday.com/tech.news/internetprivacy/2003-11-06-id-theft-tips_x.htm*

Gordon, B. (2003). *21 tips for improved wireless security.* Unpublished.

IEEE. (2001). *802.11b-1999 Wireless LANs (802.11).* Retrieved February 4, 2004, from *http://standards.ieee.org/reading/ieee/std/lanman/restricted/802.11b-1999.pdf*

Karygiannis, T., & Owens, L. (2002). *Wireless Network Security: 802.11, Bluetooth™ and handheld devices.* Retrieved February 4, 2004, from *http://csrc.nist.gov/publications/drafts/draft-sp800-48.pdf*

Kim, G., & Shin, J.G. (2003). *Proposal for a secure wireless LAN system in which the RF signal is invisible to unauthorized observers and intruders.*

Copyright © 2004, Idea Group Inc. Copying or distributing in print or electronic forms without written permission of Idea Group Inc. is prohibited.

Lewicki, R.J., & Bunker, B.B. (1996). Developing and maintaining trust in work relationships. In R.M. Kramer & T.R. Tyler (Eds.), *Trust in organizations – Frontiers of theory and research.* London: Sage Publications.

Maconachy, W., Schou, C., Ragsdale, D., & Welch, D. (2001, June 5-6). A model for information assurance: An integrated approach. *Proceedings of the 2001 IEEE Workshop on Information Assurance and Security.* Figures 1 and 2 are also taken from this paper.

Musgrove, M. (2004, February 14). Tech experts downplay theft of windows code. *Washington Post,* E1.

Nolan, R. (2001, June 29). Q&A with Harvard Business School's Dr. Richard Nolan: IT business strategies in the network era. *Harvard Business Review.*

Reid, N., & Seide, R. (2003). *802.11 (Wi-Fi) Networking Handbook* (p. 182). New York: McGraw-Hill.

Reiner, R. (Director). (1984). *This Is Spinal Tap* [Motion picture]. United States: Metro Goldwyn Mayer.

SetSolutions, Inc. (2004). Retrieved February 4, 2004 from *http://www.setsolutions.com/security.html*

Stubblefield, A., Ioannidis, J., & Rubin, A.D. (2001). *Using the Fluhrer, Mantin, and Shamir attack to break WEP* (No. TD-4ZCPZZ). AT&T Labs.

Copyright © 2004, Idea Group Inc. Copying or distributing in print or electronic forms without written permission of Idea Group Inc. is prohibited.

About the Authors

Lawrence M. Oliva is director of Infrastructure Project Management for the CSC PRIME Alliance Project, which is focused on modernizing many of the U.S. Treasury Department's communications and computing infrastructure. He has more than 25 years of experience with information security practices and procedures from both the technical and executive management perspectives, and has implemented many of the security management best practices mentioned in this book. As a certified project management professional (PMP), Oliva has managed several extraordinarily high-risk, mission-critical projects up to $160 million in budget. As vice president for a computer security firm developing biometric security solutions, his team developed and delivered procedures to quickly, securely and inexpensively migrate hundreds of financial and health care IT users from password-only conditions to multi-factor, high security biometric access environments. He is a faculty member at the University of Phoenix.

* * *

Copyright © 2004, Idea Group Inc. Copying or distributing in print or electronic forms without written permission of Idea Group Inc. is prohibited.

Chrisan Herrod is serving as both department chair of the Information Operations and Assurance Department where she is responsible for curriculum, including information security, assurance, and operations and as a professor of Information Security and Systems Management. Previously she was director of Global IT Security at GlaxoSmithKline (GSK), a large pharmaceutical company, and she was director of Information Security at Fannie Mae. While at Fannie Mae she became involved in the White House sponsored Partnership for Critical Infrastructure Security as the Information Sharing and Analysis Working Group Chair, and is currently serving as a special advisor to the Health Care Industry Information Sharing and Analysis Center initiative. She is an adjunct professor teaching information security and leadership courses with both the University of Fairfax and the University of Phoenix. From 1999 to 2001, she taught information security graduate courses at the George Washington University.

Craig E. Kaucher is a professor of Information Operations and Assurance at the National Defense University. He served in a variety of security and systems management assignments from the tactical to the strategic level, and in the U.S. Intelligence community, over a 21-year career of military service. He holds a BA in Communications from Temple University, an MS in Software Engineering Administration from Central Michigan University, and is currently pursuing a PhD in Information Systems. He also holds the Department of Defense CIO and CISO Graduate Certificates, and is a certified information security manager (CISM). He has published articles on various aspects of information security, and has spoken at numerous government and industry conferences

LTC Clifton H. Poole, CISSP, CISM, IAM, is a 20-year veteran of the U.S. Army. Clifton H. Poole currently instructs information assurance, policy development, security standards and wireless security at the Infor-

Copyright © 2004, Idea Group Inc. Copying or distributing in print or electronic forms without written permission of Idea Group Inc. is prohibited.

mation Resources Management College, National Defense University, Washington, DC. He was featured in the *Washington Post* newspaper (2003) for his research in wireless computing as he war drives the area mapping local wireless access points. He is a doctoral student in the Graduate School Computer and Information Sciences, NOVA Southeastern University.

Charles Rex IV is the chief information officer and director of academic operations at the National War College in Washington, DC. He received a bachelor's degree from the Virginia Military Institute, an MBA from the University of Phoenix, and holds the chief information officer certification and Information Assurance certification from the Information Resources Management College at the National Defense University. Mr. Rex owns a business consulting firm and is a member of the faculty at the University of Phoenix.

Copyright © 2004, Idea Group Inc. Copying or distributing in print or electronic forms without written permission of Idea Group Inc. is prohibited.

Index

Copyright © 2004, Idea Group Inc. Copying or distributing in print or electronic forms without written permission of Idea Group Inc. is prohibited.

Copyright © 2004, Idea Group Inc. Copying or distributing in print or electronic forms without written permission of Idea Group Inc. is prohibited.

Copyright © 2004, Idea Group Inc. Copying or distributing in print or electronic forms without written permission of Idea Group Inc. is prohibited.

30-DAY FREE TRIAL!

InfoSci-Online Database

www.infosci-online.com

Provide instant access to the latest offerings of Idea Group Inc. publications in the fields of INFORMATION SCIENCE, TECHNOLOGY and MANAGEMENT

During the past decade, with the advent of telecommunications and the availability of distance learning opportunities, more college and university libraries can now provide access to comprehensive collections of research literature through access to online databases.

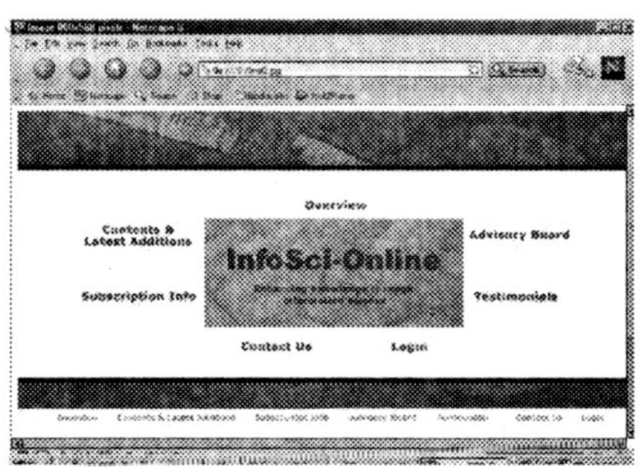

The InfoSci-Online database is the most comprehensive collection of ***full-text*** literature regarding research, trends, technologies, and challenges in the fields of information science, technology and management. This online database consists of over 3000 book chapters, 200+ journal articles, 200+ case studies and over 1,000+ conference proceedings papers from IGI's three imprints (Idea Group Publishing, Information Science Publishing and IRM Press) that can be accessed by users of this database through identifying areas of research interest and keywords.

Contents & Latest Additions:
Unlike the delay that readers face when waiting for the release of print publications, users will find this online database updated as soon as the material becomes available for distribution, providing instant access to the latest literature and research findings published by Idea Group Inc. in the field of information science and technology, in which emerging technologies and innovations are constantly taking place, and where time is of the essence.

The content within this database will be updated by IGI with 1300 new book chapters, 250+ journal articles and case studies and 250+ conference proceedings papers per year, all related to aspects of information, science, technology and management, published by Idea Group Inc. The updates will occur as soon as the material becomes available, even before the publications are sent to print.

InfoSci-Online pricing flexibility allows this database to be an excellent addition to your library, regardless of the size of your institution.

Contact: 717-533-8845 (Ext. 10), cust@idea-group.com for a 30-day trial subscription to InfoSci-Online.

A product of:

INFORMATION SCIENCE PUBLISHING*
Enhancing Knowledge Through Information Science
http://www.info-sci-pub.com

**an imprint of Idea Group Inc.*